The
Square
Mile

The Square Mile

The City of London in colour

Terence Coen
and
Alec Forshaw

B.T. Batsford Ltd, London

ISBN 0 7134 5400 8

Printed in Hong Kong
for the publishers
B. T. Batsford Ltd.
4 Fitzhardinge Street
London W1H 0AH

Frontispiece: Winter in the City

Contents

1

Introduction

London is one of the world's great cities. Its administrative boundaries, comprising the thirty-two London boroughs, contain seven million people and embrace 610 square miles. Beyond these boundaries the built-up area spreads even deeper into the territory of Kent, Surrey, Buckinghamshire, Hertfordshire and Essex.

At the centre of this enormous, sprawling metropolis lies the City of London, a mere 1.03 square miles, 0.16% of the Greater London area, and with a resident population of only 7,000 people, just one Londoner out of every thousand. Looking at a map of London, the City is a tiny dot in the middle, like the minute core of a fruit which has expanded uncontrollably and inexorably over the centuries.

What is surprising is that despite this staggering and almost freakish growth, the City has retained functions and influence far out of proportion to its limited physical size. While the central quarter of many ancient continental cities is now a quaintly preserved or meticulously reconstructed precinct of historic buildings, given over to tourists, couriers, and ice-cream sellers, the City of London remains the densest concentration of commercial activity and business tradition in all London.

The City is the kernel where London began, a seed sown by the Romans nearly 2,000 years ago. For three-quarters of its life London was the City, confined until Tudor times to the land within the old Roman walls. Beyond these defences, repaired and reinforced by Saxons and Normans, market gardens, meadows, marshlands and woods extended out towards untamed heaths and forests. Only in the last 500 years has London burst free of these shackles. Since then the City has been the epicentre from

which shock-waves of bricks and mortar have rippled out into the countryside – the aristocratic squares of the grand Georgian and Regency estates in the West End, the docks and industries in the east, the solid terraces and villas of the Victorian and Edwardian suburbs and the far-reaching tentacles of twentieth-century metroland.

Above all else, the City is a market place. London originated as a port, the highest point up the Thames estuary easily navigable for sea-going ships and the lowest bridging point across the river. While the physical importing and exporting of goods is no longer important, the City markets, together with the service industries of insurance, merchant banking and broking, have evolved and expanded to deal with almost every conceivable commodity. Unchanging, however, is the spirit of trust and co-operation throughout all the City markets. 'My word is my bond' remains the basis and strength of City trading.

Impressively and determinedly the City has won, maintained and enhanced its standing as the financial and trading centre of the capital, the nation and arguably the world. It has kept its independence and its power by a mixture of shrewdness and sound judgement and an eye to the future – a successful combination of traditional conservatism and a willingness to adapt to the present.

New buildings have risen on the rubble of the old, each time meeting the requirements of a new century. Today the thirty-storey Stock Exchange and the 600-foot tower of the National Westminster Bank soar skywards just a few paces from where the Romans laid out their forum or market place, from where Sir Thomas Gresham built his Royal Exchange in 1571, and from the coffee houses where insurance, banking and broking were born.

Historic buildings which have escaped the ravages of fire and bomb have been preserved where possible but have not stood in the way of progress. The City has not become a fossilised

The stone pinnacles of St. Michael's Cornhill once stood out proudly against the City skyline, but are now overshadowed by the massive tower of the National Westminster Bank.

museum, but presents a modern face. Dick Whittington, Samuel Pepys, Christopher Wren, or even Sir Herbert Baker who redesigned the Bank of England in 1921, would be shocked if they could see it now.

The City has many facets, and means different things to different people. Of the 350,000 men and women who work in the City, the 7,000 residents who live there, or the tens of thousands of Londoners who watch the Lord Mayor's Show or visit the Barbican Arts Centre, each has a particular image of the City. To some it is the mystique of big business and multi-national banks, or the secure financial and commercial bastions of the Bank of England, the Stock Exchange and Lloyd's. To others it is the majestic dome of St. Paul's Cathedral, the reassuring sword and scales of Justice at the Old Bailey, the chattering newsprint of Fleet Street, or the solemn legal enclaves of the Temple.

Some people will have favourite lunchtime watering holes, or churchyards to sit in on sunny days. Yet one wonders how much even the privileged ones, those familiar with the inside of a livery company hall, see or know of the City, its market places, customs, ceremonies and curiosities. How many passers-by ever raise their eyes above pavement level to marvel at the elegance of Wren's church spires or the awesome height of the blocks which dwarf them?

Behind its main thoroughfares, the City retains a capillary network of narrow alleyways and courtyards. Nestling beneath office blocks, old pubs, hostelries and company halls squeeze into tight corners and eccentrically shaped churches hide postage-stamp graveyards. The quiet backwaters of Cloth Fair, Carter Lane, Crutched Friars and Bow Lane hold the charm of the old City. Those who hurtle in cars down Lower Thames Street or London Wall see nothing but brash exteriors of glass and concrete. The tourists who whistle-stop to St. Paul's and the Tower from Buckingham Palace and Westminster Abbey miss the essential qualities of the City.

This book is a contemporary and personal view of the City. It is not a formal history or an official guide. The photographs are images of the City today. The text complements this portrayal of the City's strange beauty with a feel for its past and the weight of history which has

St. Paul's Cathedral, Wren's masterpiece, viewed across the River Thames from Waterloo Bridge.

fashioned the practices and privileges of this remarkable place. Urban dwellers are often comforted by Samuel Johnson's famous remark: 'He who tires of London tires of life'. One could also suggest that he who tires of the City tires of London. First, however, one must get to know it in order to love it. It is an engrossing and consuming adventure.

Part of the panorama from the public viewing gallery of the Monument looking south-east towards HMS Belfast, _now permanently moored on the Thames._

A pigeon's view from St. Paul's Cathedral into the churchyard.

2
Gateways to the City

It is easy to visit or even live in London without ever setting foot in the City. The compactness of the City contrasts starkly with the monstrous extent of London. From the vantage points of Hampstead Heath, Archway Road, Blackheath or Crystal Palace, either side of the Thames valley, the whole of the City from the comforting dome of St. Paul's to the pencil stubs of the Barbican and Nat-West towers can almost be grasped in one hand, while suburbia sprawls to every horizon.

The precise boundaries of the City are less simple to follow today than they once were. For centuries, the Roman walls formed an unmistakable division between town and country. From Ludgate, Newgate, Aldersgate, Cripplegate, Bishopsgate and Aldgate, roads radiated to nearby villages and distant towns. A seventh gate, Moorgate, was added in medieval times and the others enlarged or rebuilt to provide lodgings, taverns, or in the case of Newgate an infamous prison. The surviving gates at York or Canterbury indicate what they were like – statuesque, impregnable, and incredible bottlenecks for traffic. As traffic increased their survival became impossible; they were demolished in 1760, not before time. Large sections of the City wall disappeared also.

In the Middle Ages the jurisdiction of the City was extended north and west to include the extramural suburbs or 'liberties' of Smithfield, Holborn and the Temple. New boundaries were marked by 'bars' across the roads, wooden barriers closed at night and patrolled during the day to prevent the entry of vagrants, vagabonds and unauthorised traders. Temple Bar was rebuilt after the Great Fire by Christopher Wren as an ornate triple arch. It survived in situ until 1878 as 'a bone in the throat of Fleet Street'. Conservationists ensured its re-erection in less congested surroundings in Theobald's Park. Now it is to be returned to the City, controversially close to St. Paul's, not in Fleet Street.

Today the City's entrances are guarded by the griffons and dragons which appear on the City shield, symbolically warding off any evil spirits foolish enough to approach. In places, the boundary meanders anachronistically through the middle of buildings, where once there were alleyways. Some tenants pay rates to several authorities!

The biggest boundary of the City is the river. Originally it was much shallower and wider, rich with salmon and oyster beds. In 1250 a Norwegian bear, part of the Royal Menagerie kept at the Tower, used to wade into the Thames to fish, tethered by a chain. By 1500 the river was badly polluted, its fish suffocated. However, it had become the High Street of London, the City's commercial life-line, packed with boats of every description – ocean galleons, rowing barques, hay barges, skiffs and ferries. In the last century steam replaced sail – colliers, coasters, tramps and trawlers, tugs and lighters, even paddle steamers taking daytrippers to Southend.

The wharves of Garlickhythe, Queenhythe and Bear Quay were crucial entrypoints into the City. With the demise of London's docks, river traffic has dwindled to a few barges carrying rubbish and tourist pleasure boats. Thames watermen are a select band, their hythes and jetties idle.

The five bridges remain vital gateways into the City, three carrying roads and two railways. The oldest and most famous is London Bridge, though the present structure is the newest and dullest. The massive timber bulkheads of the original wooden bridge have recently been unearthed at Billingsgate. The first stone bridge, built in 1176, was one of the wonders of the

Griffons mark the City's boundary at all its major approaches, supposedly warding off evil spirits. (overleaf)

Southwark Bridge is the narrowest and least used of the five bridges which cross the River Thames into the City. (overleaf)

medieval world, the greatest engineering feat since Roman times. 910 feet long and only twenty feet wide it had nineteen arches and soon became cluttered with three and four storey houses which projected over the sides. Peter de Colechurch, the designer, was buried in the chapel to Thomas à Becket which served as a shrine on the bridge for Canterbury pilgrims. The church of St. Magnus the Martyr stood at the north end while the severed heads of criminals and traitors were spiked onto the southern portcullis. By 1358 there were 138 shops on the bridge, restricting the road width to fifteen feet. The narrow arches acted like a sluice and erosion by the tidal flow required constant repairs of the supports – London Bridge was often falling down. Nonetheless it stood for 650 years. Like its builder, the senior partner of the contractors who demolished the old bridge in 1831 was a cleric, hence the saying 'one priest put it here and another priest took it down'.

Rennie's elegant rusticated bridge which replaced it lasted until 1971 when it too had to make way for a wider, stronger bridge. An American oil corporation paid £1 million for the satisfaction of moving Rennie's bridge to Arizona, helping to defray the £7.5 million cost of the new bridge.

Blackfriars Bridge was constructed in 1760, just losing the race with Westminster Bridge to be London's second river crossing. The present structure, designed by James Cubitt, was finished in 1869, complete with pulpit piers and splendid ironwork. Its width, 110 feet, was greater than any other in Britain at the time.

Southwark Bridge is the least used of all the Thames bridges, and rather difficult to get at from either end. Originally a private tollbridge it was bought and remodelled by the City Corporation. They also built Tower Bridge, just outside the City, but one of London's great landmarks. (Rumour has it that the Americans believed they were buying Tower Bridge!) All four bridges are maintained entirely at the City Corporation's expense. The Bridge House Estates Fund pre-dates the Norman conquest. Hundreds of City wills contained a sum to 'God and the Bridge', so many in fact that there is now an annual investment income of £4.5 million.

The two railway bridges into Holborn Viaduct and Cannon Street carry equally large numbers of people each day. Together with the other termini – Liverpool Street, Fenchurch Street and Moorgate – and the numerous underground stations, they are twice-daily flooded with commuters. The twin towers of Cannon Street form a grand portal. Ironically the glass roof was destroyed while in safe-keeping during the war, and never replaced. On the South Bank thou-

sands disembark at London Bridge Station and pour across the bridge. Pity anyone struggling against the morning flow! Better to turn and follow the surge.

Behind Blackfriars Bridge the eastern half of the City is dominated by the National Westminster Tower: on the right are the maintenance gantries on top of Richard Rogers' new Lloyd's building.

3
Roman London

Before the Romans there was no London. They founded Londinium for a specific purpose in a carefully selected site. The Roman Empire was based on the establishment and authority of cities. Of the thousand European, African and Asian cities founded by Rome, London excels. Never did the Romans choose a better site, not even Rome itself. No other Roman city has subsequently been so successful and prosperous.

It can scarcely have seemed likely to Claudius' invading army in AD 43. Having crossed the Medway after a bloody two-day battle the weary legionaries reached a disheartening obstacle, a marshy valley drained by a wide, muddy, meandering river. The retreating Britons fled across the Thames by an ancient ford, near Westminster. The Roman sappers decided to build a pontoon bridge on a more direct north-south line, further downstream. The bridgehead was consolidated with defensive positions on the north bank and a southern bulwark (Southwark). After a short delay Claudius marched north to take the British stronghold at Colchester and to win decisive battles at Chester and Cirencester. Within a few months lowland Britain was conquered.

The temporary pontoon was replaced by permanent wooden piles and piers. From the north bank new roads were built radiating to the frontier military bases at York, Lincoln and Gloucester. Watling, Ermine, Stane and Akeman Streets were the life-lines of Roman control. The hub of this network, the Thames bridge, was the obvious place for a supply port. The river was navigatable as far as the bridge; Londinium became the maritime gateway for Roman Britain.

Settlement on the north rather than the south bank was favoured by two dry gravel hills (Cornhill and Ludgate), divided by the small Walbrook and bordered on the west by the larger Fleet river. Merchants, businessmen and traffickers rapidly established an important trade centre for imports and exports, integrating the new province into the economy of the

empire. Not surprisingly Boudicca and her Iceni rebels, triumphant after the sacking of Colchester, turned on London to vent their wrath against a symbol of alien civilisation and wealth. Fearing a repetition of the massacre of the ninth legion Suetonius evacuated his troops, leaving the Roman bourgeoisie and British collaborators to an atrocious fate. When the victorious fourteenth and twentieth legions returned after a defeating Boudicca north of St. Albans they encountered a scene of vindictive annihilation, every building razed, the ground strewn with the severed members of 15,000 corpses. The first London had lasted only seventeen years; the earliest archaeological evidence is a thick layer of ash and the dozen beheaded skulls dug out of the bed of the Walbrook near the Mansion House.

The Romans quickly re-established London, this time on a firmer basis. After 60 AD new buildings were mainly stone; London soon became the provincial capital. During the second and third centuries this cosmopolitan centre of commerce and politics blossomed as the web of imperial trade expanded and Roman bureaucracy proliferated. Rather like the British Raj, the Roman system proved immediately valid for the indigenous population, who were integrated into the hierarchy. Beside the river the 'civil service' buildings of Government House occupied five acres, larger than the present British Museum. The London Stone, still preserved in the wall of the Bank of China in Cannon Street, stood in the main gateway, probably a milestone from which distances were measured. The basilica (town hall) took up one side of the forum (market place) between Gracechurch and Lime Streets. From here public works were ordered, laws approved and regulations administered. Its foundations were meticulously recorded when

The fragment of Roman Wall at Cooper's Row is the tallest and most authentic relic of the original City defences.

Leadenhall was rebuilt in 1881 – 500 feet long, 200 feet wide, almost the size of St. Paul's. A further dig in 1986 yielded fresh evidence.

A regimented grid of streets was laid out. Wealth from the prosperous trade in corn, wine, tin and leather enabled the construction of lavish villas, public baths and schools. A monumental arch was built in 122 AD to celebrate Hadrian's campaigns. The statue's head was later hacked from its body and hurled into the Thames where in 1830 it was rediscovered, miraculously preserved in mud.

The location of other major buildings such as the amphitheatre and hippodrome which must have existed in a city of 100,000 people is unknown. The main surviving evidence of Roman endeavour is the defensive wall, begun in 200 AD. This massive venture incorporated the rectangular fort at the Barbican and enclosed 330 acres, an area exceeded only by Rome, Milan and Nimes. Two miles long, twenty feet high and nine feet wide, its construction was supervised by the garrison of 1,500 soldiers using slave labour. 1,300 barge-loads of Kentish ragstone were floated from Maidstone to face the rubble-filled wall, bonded with regular courses of flat tiles. Excellent sections of wall are visible at London Wall, Noble Street, Cooper's Row and Minories, and from the Museum of London. The wall's route can be traced by the twenty-one information panels placed at strategic intervals.

Few other obvious reminders of Roman London survive. Apart from the gateway roads their street pattern disappeared together with all their splendid buildings. Excavations for redevelopment, however, constantly throw up artefacts and relics. In 1805 a complete tessellated floor, now in the British Museum, was unearthed on the site of the Bank of England. The construction of Queen Victoria Street in 1869 exposed the Bucklersbury mosaic, now beautifully displayed in the Museum of London. Most spectacular was the discovery in 1954 during foundation works for Bucklersbury House of the Temple of Mithras, built in 240 AD on the banks of the Walbrook. The remains were painstakingly reconstructed beside the new offices for public view. It measures 58 × 26 feet, with an apse rather like a Christian church. Mithraism, however, was a severe, ritualistic and fatalistic religion, heresy to the central doctrine of Christianity. Christian iconoclasts ransacked the Mithraeum and buried the exquisite marble head, now in the Museum of London. The site of the first Christian church in Roman London is uncertain – perhaps St. Peter's Cornhill or St. Alban's Wood Street. St. Paul's was a Saxon foundation.

The Roman occupation ended as rapidly as it began. In 410 AD the Vandals overran Italy and the emperor in Constantinople recalled his colonial legions. London was left to defend itself. The Romanised civilians hired German mercenaries to repel raiders, but in vain. The British armies retreated to their ancient trackways and hillforts where King Arthur, last of the Roman generals, waged a rearguard campaign. During the misty obscurity of the Dark Ages Roman roads and towns were abandoned. London was bypassed in the struggle for territory; for a while organised urban life ceased.

The extensive sections of patched-up wall at the Barbican have been cleverly and carefully incorporated into the redevelopment.

4
Before the Fire

The Romans had proved that London was an ideal site for a city. Before long new settlers reoccupied the Roman shell and began to fashion the City we know today. By 650 AD London was the main town of the East Saxons, who controlled Essex, and soon came under the rule of Mercia and the Middle Saxons. Wessex remained the political and military battleground – Winchester was the seat of English kings until William the Conqueror built the Tower and set up court in Westminster. Left to its own devices Saxon London developed as a seaport and mercantile centre, largely self-governing. Within the protective Roman walls a wooden shanty-town mushroomed. The basis of today's street plan evolved.

Unlike imperial Londinium the medieval City had no central square or systematic grid pattern. From the Tower to Baynard Castle near Ludgate the riverside was crammed with quays and tall narrow warehouses of weather-boarded timber, coated with pitch. Wharves like Garlickhythe handled particular goods – garlic was the favourite spice for disguising the taste of rancid meat! Similarly, different trades clustered in particular streets within the City, still remembered in modern street names – Bread Street, Milk Street, Wood Street, Poultry Street, Cannon (corrupted from Candlewick) Street, Ropemaker Street, Ironmonger Lane, French Ordinary Court, Sea-coal Lane. Craftsmen with common interests formed guilds and companies.

The widest street was used for the main market, or ceap; Cheapside remains the principal shopping street in the City. Friday Street held a once-weekly fish market to supplement Billingsgate and Fish Street Hill. Unfortunately Victorian and Edwardian euphemists replaced the less salubrious names of the old butchers' shambles: Blow Bladder Lane became Newgate Street, Stinking Lane was rechristened King Edward Street!

Immigrants were attracted. Jews, disbarred from citizenship, were encouraged by strong Christian taboos into money lending, although allegations of usury incited racial harassment. In the pogrom of 1262 their synagogue in Old Jewry was sacked and 700 people died. They were expelled by Edward I in 1290 and not welcomed back until Oliver Cromwell's Commonwealth. (Shakespeare had never met a Jew when he portrayed Shylock.) Florentine and Milanese merchants took their place, settling in Lombard Street. Each shop displayed distinctive signs – the unicorn, star, fox, white horse, grasshopper and golden fleece. The Lombards introduced systems of paper transactions and their benches ('banco' in Italian) dispensed documents of credit and bills of exchange. Banks were born.

Where Cannon Street station stands the Hanseatic league of Baltic merchants, known as Eastlings, had their 'staelhof' or staple house, oddly corrupted to Steel Yard. Their insistence on payment in highest quality gold spawned the term 'sterling'. Their monopoly caused resentment and they were evicted by Elizabeth I.

By then London was beginning to dominate world trade. Dutch rivalry was weakened by wars with Spain. Merchant adventurers like Willoughby and Chancellor opened new trade links. In 1599 the East India Company was formed. Twenty-eight years earlier Sir Thomas Gresham had built the Royal Exchange, emulating Antwerp's bourse. The courtyard, and its arcade of 200 shops provided a central meeting place for merchants, a successor to the Roman forum. Sandwiched between Cornhill and Threadneedle Street the tall cupola tower was capped by Gresham's grasshopper emblem.

Vast amounts of money and energy were poured into ecclesiastical buildings. Religion and superstition ruled the daily lives and outlook of medieval society – the equivalent of

Lombard Street takes its name from the Italian merchants who introduced the idea of banking to the City in the fourteenth century.

twentieth-century materialism. Large precincts inside and outside the walls accommodated religious orders – Greyfriars and St. Bartholomew's Priory near Newgate, White and Crutched Friars in the east, Blackfriars and the Knights Templar either side of the Fleet beside the river. The beautiful Norman chancel of the Priory church of St. Bartholomew-the-Great reminds us of the devotion and skill of that age. By 1600 109 parish churches had been built in the City, in a variety of Saxon, Norman, Early English and Perpendicular styles. Many were financed by the immense wealth derived from wool which similarly funded the magnificent churches of East Anglia and Somerset where the sheep were reared. St. Olave, Hart Street, St. Andrew Undershaft and St. Helen's Bishopgate are outstanding survivors.

The City skyline, bristling with towers and turrets, was dominated by St. Paul's Cathedral. In the presence of Wren's masterpiece it is often forgotten that its predecessor was one of the greatest Gothic cathedrals; 585 feet long, crowned by a majestic spire 449 feet high, and roofed with six acres of lead, it was the largest and tallest building in Europe until Milan and Seville cathedrals were completed. The east end contained a gigantic rose window. Dr. Wren had been appointed in 1660 to supervise restoration. He clearly loathed Gothic architecture – 'thick walls without judgement, great pillars without any graceful manner'. Perhaps he would have criticised Wells or Chartres similarly. Fortunately we were spared his plan to bridge the Norman nave and Early English choir with a renaissance dome. Outside the Cathedral, lath and plaster houses crowded against the flying buttresses. The nave was used as a market and thoroughfare to bypass the convoluted alleys. At Corpus Christi the procession circumambulated the cathedral; the creed was chanted in Creed Lane, the Hail Mary in Ave Maria Lane, the Lord's Prayer in Paternoster Row, the amens in Amen Court.

The lack of substantial open space within the walls forced land-hungry activities outside – the livestock market at Smithfield, the annual Cloth Fair, sport and recreation at Moorfields, plays and pageants at Clerkenwell, executions at Tower Hill and Smithfield. Despite the calamitous Black Death when two-fifths of Londoners died, and repeated outbreaks of bubonic plague,

population expanded. By Tudor times the City had broken its shackles and extended its boundaries to include the liberties. Ribbon development hugged the tracks to Whitechapel, Islington, Hoxton and Westminster. The chronicler John Stow whose memorial stands in St. Andrew Undershaft lamented the building of houses on meadows where he had played as a boy.

William Fitzstephen eulogised London as 'the most noble of cities', 'a pleasant, merry place'. Foreigners admired the fine churches and marvelled at London Bridge. Above the forest of spires, kites and rooks wheeled in the sky. Such glowing accounts must be tempered by the reality of London life – congested, squalid, disease-ridden, brutal and uncompassionate. The savage penal system administered 200 separate offences punishable by death. Strict curfews were necessary to curb the street crime on which the handicapped and disadvantaged depended. Daniel Defoe described the ditches around the walls.

These filthy places receive all the sinks and drains from dye-houses, wash houses, fell-mongers, slaughter-houses, and all kinds of offensive trades. They are continually full of carrion and the most odious of all stench proceeds from them as to make people loth to pass them.

We have come some way since then.

The grasshopper was the emblem of Sir Thomas Gresham who in 1571 built the first Royal Exchange between Cornhill and Threadneedle Street and established London as the world's financial capital.

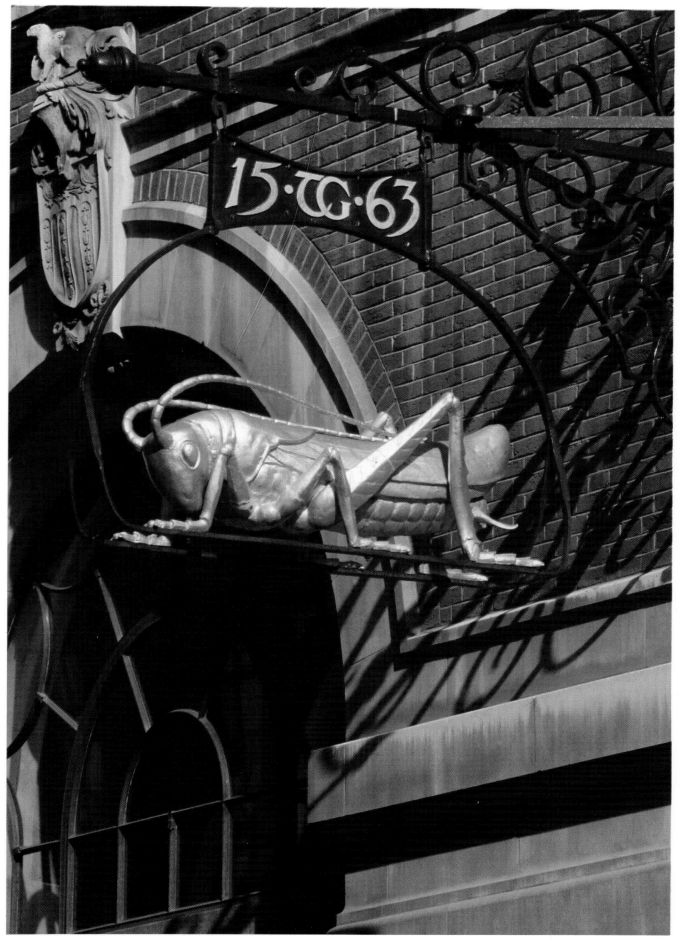

Fishmongers' Hall, one of the finest livery company halls, fronts the river beside London Bridge.

5
Guilds and Livery Companies

The City livery companies are the most durable inheritance from medieval London. Although outsiders might regard them as fortresses of pageant and prestige, where patrimonial and old-school ties are over-important, they represent a remarkably continuous link with the guilds of the Middle Ages, and still play a prominent part in City life.

Their origins extend back to early Saxon friths and 'gilds' when men of a particular craft or 'mystery' formed associations to control trade, establish rules and protect their interests from outside competition. Individual craftsmen congregated in distinct quarters in the City, sharing strong common bonds. The guilds, through regular contributions from their members, introduced systems of mutual aid and set up regulations for their trade and workforce. After a seven year apprenticeship craftsmen became masters or journeymen (paid on a day or 'journée' basis). Their respectability ensured that they became a crucial part of society, fulfilling vital civic duties. The more prosperous guilds built company halls to meet in and had their own liveries and uniforms for special occasions.

The Weavers claim to be the oldest, or at least the first to receive a charter, in 1164. In return for money paid to the king, royal charters conferred privileges and monopolies on the company, thus increasing their power and wealth. In 1305 the Vintners were guaranteed the Gascony wine trade by Edward I, a windfall still celebrated by their annual procession on a July Thursday from Vintners Hall to St. James's Garlickhythe. A vanguard of wine porters sweep the streets 'lest they do slip in the mire or their nostrils be offended by malodours'!

The Parish Clerks (who like the Watermen never took a livery) were the second to obtain a charter, in 1232, followed by the Saddlers in 1280, the Mercers in 1303, the Bakers in 1307, the Skinners and Goldsmiths in 1327. Restrictive practices and inter-guild disputes resulted in a struggle for supremacy among different companies, sometimes involving violent feuds.

Eventually a pecking order emerged, based on wealth rather than age. In 1515 a top echelon of twelve was decreed by the Lord Mayor – the Mercers, Grocers, Drapers, Fishmongers, Goldsmiths, Skinners, Merchant Taylors, Haberdashers, Slaters, Ironmongers, Vintners and Clothworkers. The long-standing rivalry of the Skinners and Merchant Taylors was resolved by alternating places – hence our expression 'at sixes and sevens'. Five of the twelve were in the wool and cloth trade which dominated the medieval economy. In 1275 a special levy on raw wool encouraged weaving in the wool areas for sale and export in London. In 1480 a million yards of cloth were taxed at Customs House. The Mercers, of whom Dick Whittington was a notable member, took their cut.

Extravagant feasting became commonplace among the richer companies who vied with each other in their splendour and expense. In 1607 the Merchant Taylors spent £1,000 on one evening entertaining James I and his court. It proved money well spent as his son and several noblemen subsequently became freemen and donated funds in their wills. When toasting the monarch the Vintners still give five, rather than three, cheers, dating from the occasion when they entertained five kings to dinner. The rituals of admission and promotion within the companies were reminiscent of the Mastersingers of Nuremberg. On Midsummer Eve all the City companies wore their finest livery for the procession of the Night Watch through the streets. Rembrandt painted the Dutch equivalent.

The companies reached the zenith of their political power in Tudor times. The disasters of the seventeenth century – civil war, plague and fire – emptied their coffers, divided their loyalties, usurped their power and destroyed their halls. Wealth was restored in the eighteenth century. but never the monopolistic grip on the reins of commerce. Gradually the guilds lost their trade-union image. Bequests were channelled into promoting education, charities and the arts, whilst maintaining the private ceremonies and

Each livery company has its own colourful shield; the College of Arms in Upper Thames Street administers and registers all the nation's heraldry.

comforts of their City premises. The leading companies established schools, partly for the members' own offspring, partly philanthropic. The Mercers founded St. Paul's School in 1509 for 153 boys (supposedly the number of fish caught in St. Peter's net). In 1884 they greatly enlarged it on a new site in Hammersmith. Similarly the Grocers founded Oundle and the Skinners, Tonbridge. All have now left the City – Haberdashers Aske's and Merchant Taylors to Hertfordshire – including even Christ's Hospital and Charterhouse (which began in monastic institutions). The livery companies still contribute scholarships, governors and pupils. Numerous almshouses and charitable trusts, spread countrywide, are maintained. Many City churches are adopted and supported by a livery company.

Today there are ninety-six livery companies, of which nineteen received charters this century. Two of the newcomers are surprisingly ancient professions – the Farmers and Furniture Makers. The Airline Pilots and Navigators, Actuaries, Arbitrators, Chartered Accountants and Chartered Surveyors are more predictable additions.

Although the great livery companies now have few links with their original medieval trades several still perform long-established duties and preserve ancient traditions. In Goldsmiths' Hall silver, gold and the coins of the realm are tested in the Trial of Pyx (hence the term hallmark to denote a metal's integrity). Fishmongers still vet the quality of fish at New Billingsgate, and the Gunsmiths proof firearms. The Spectacle Makers and Apothecaries grant diplomas to opticians and chemists. Several companies now embrace their modern successors, such as the Fanmakers and the ventilation industry, the Coachmakers and the car manufacturers. Some ceremonies, however, are decidedly archaic. The Butchers each January present a boar's head to the Lord Mayor. The Dyers and Vintners maintain the custom of Swan Upping on the Thames, marking new cygnets to distinguish them from the royal birds. More significantly the City liverymen still elect the sheriff, aldermen and senior officers of the City Corporation. From their ranks they select the Lord Mayor.

Thirty-seven companies still have halls in the City. The Merchant Taylors remain on their original site in Threadneedle Street (the three needles of their emblem). So do the Skinners in Garlick Hill, near the Beaver House auction rooms, and the Fishmongers near Billingsgate. Though frequently hidden away and unostentatious from outside, behind their gates and doorways lie sumptuous interiors, grand staircases lit by sparkling chandeliers and magnificent dining rooms where port is passed in silver decanters. Associated with their liveries, though not actually a company, is the College of Arms, founded in 1484 to administer and register armorial bearings and heraldic badges. It remains a most remarkable institution, imbued with the romance and riddles of shields, crests and pennants.

Whatever one's view of the exclusiveness or quaintness of the livery companies they undoubtedly take their responsibilities seriously and uphold their traditions with careful pride. Their constitutional stability ensures a quiet dignity and wise charity, rarely found elsewhere.

6
The Great Fire

It had been a long hot summer; the threat of plague which had killed 56,558 Londoners the previous year hung over the City. When a small fire broke out at 2 a.m. on Sunday 2nd September 1666 in a bakery in Pudding Lane off Eastcheap nobody was much concerned. Sir Thomas Bludworth, the Lord Mayor, inspected the blaze at 3 a.m. Dismissively he remarked 'a woman might piss it out', and returned to bed. He failed to appreciate the fierce east wind fanning the flames. Nearby the tightly-spaced wooden warehouses and shops were tinder dry, mostly locked for the sabbath. The fire spread rapidly south-west and north-west, racing wildly along the river frontage.

By the time Samuel Pepys alerted the oblivious Charles II at Westminster it was too late. Firebreaks were leapt by sparks, which even crossed the river to start fires in Southwark. Panic-stricken citizens scrambled hysterically to evacuate their personal possessions. Racketeers hired out carts at exorbitant prices. The hapless Bludworth despaired – 'Lord, what can I do?' Pepys abandoned his house in Seething Lane (having buried his wine in the garden) and took to the river.

> When we could endure no more upon the water, we to a little alehouse on Bankside, and saw the fire grow; and in corners and upon steeples, and between churches and houses, as far as we could see up the hill of the City, in a most horrid, malicious, bloody flame. We stayed till, it being darkish, we saw the fire as only one entire arch of above a mile long; it made me weep to see it.

John Evelyn documented the sight – 'All the sky were of a fiery aspect, like the top of a burning oven, and the light seen forty miles round about.'

The smoke pall dimmed the sun in Oxford; charred paper landed in Windsor.

The Paternoster Row booksellers sought sanctuary in St. Paul's to save their stock. Alas, timber scaffolding caught and ignited the roof. Molten lead poured down the walls into the streets. 'The very pavements glowed with redness. Neither horse nor man was able to tread on them' (Evelyn). Stone columns and buttresses exploded in the heat like grenades. Boulders of Caen stone plunged through the nave into the crypt, crammed with books.

The fire raged for four days, destroying 13,200 houses and eighty-nine churches; 436 acres, measuring $1\frac{1}{2}$ miles long by $\frac{1}{2}$ mile wide, were devastated. Eastwards the flames moved slowly against the wind and were eventually blocked by Leadenhall. St. Helen's and St. Ethelburga Bishopsgate survived. The Court evacuated Westminster but the City walls checked the inferno at Smithfield, saving St. Bartholomew's. In Giltspur Street the gilded Fat Boy of Pye Corner marks the fire's limit, a warning against the gluttony which 'caused' the catastrophe. Amazingly, only four people died, including the baker's maidservant. Another had huddled beside St. Paul's, every limb reduced to charcoal. More died later from shock and from falling into basements while sifting through the ruins. Medieval London had perished; the laborious process of rebuilding lay ahead.

Sir Christopher Wren's monument to the Great Fire of London 1666, 202 feet high and erected 202 feet from where the fire started in Pudding Lane.

*The bas-relief at the foot of the Monument depicts the
terror of the fire, and the heroism of the King and his
fire-fighters.*

7
Wren's City

It was November before the water supply was reconnected; smouldering cellars continued to flare up until the following March. Among the ashes temporary booths and tents were erected – a courtroom operated from the shell of the Guildhall. Yet within two weeks of the Fire, while the pavements were still cooling, Evelyn had drawn bold plans for reconstructing the City, with five spacious squares linked by an east-west boulevard. The young Christopher Wren – mathematician, astronomer and architect – also presented plans, keeping St. Paul's and the Royal Exchange as focal points within a brand-new street grid, banishing obnoxious industries to eastern suburbs.

Wren's utopian ideas impressed his friend, Charles II, but proved impractical. Speed was everything; 100,000 refugees were camping out in the fields, merchants were impatient to rebuild quickly before trade was lost to rival ports. Legal wrangles over redistributing land were interminable. Apart from limited road widening, the City was rebuilt on its medieval street pattern. New legislation at least demanded brick and stone, and banned projecting timber. The wooden oriels of Nos. 41–2 Cloth Fair are rare examples of pre-Fire houses. By 1673 12,000 homes had been built, including those in the expanding West End. Wren's town planning dreams were frustrated.

Nevertheless Wren was appointed Surveyor General of the King's Works and commissioned to rebuild fifty-one of the 112 City parish churches (twenty-three had survived undamaged and thirty-eight were abandoned altogether), and St. Paul's Cathedral, the biggest prize. Funds were raised by a special coal tax, divided three ways between St. Paul's, the churches and house owners. For once the restrictive rules of the guilds had to be waived as provincial craftsmen and labourers were drafted in to tackle the massive task. (The tax on coal survived until repealed by Lord Randolph Churchill, Sir Winston's father. Coal meanwhile took its revenge by blackening the facades of St. Paul's and the other churches!)

Hopes of repairing the burnt-out nave of St. Paul's were dashed by a collapse of masonry in April 1668. It was decided to start afresh. 47,000 cartloads of stone were dismantled and taken for the parish churches. Only one object from old St. Paul's survived, the tomb of John Donne who was dean for the last ten years of his life, having recanted his youthful excesses.

Wren's blueprint was approved in time for construction to commence in 1675. The project engrossed him for the next thirty-five years. From his house at Cardinal's Wharf near Bear Gardens in Southwark he could survey the whole length of the City. He visited St. Paul's daily, supervising the masons, instructing the foremen, modifying the details of his design. In the later stages he regularly climbed the 450-foot-high dome, despite his age, to inspect the work. Wren's renaissance masterpiece used 50,000 tons of Portland stone, 25,000 tons of limestone, 11,000 tons of ragstone, 1000 tons of chalk and 500 tons of marble. The great dome is no simple copy of St. Peter's Rome – Wren in fact never travelled further afield than Paris. This miraculous timber structure smoothly skinned with lead remains London's finest landmark. Those who climb to its famous Whispering Gallery are rewarded with breathtaking views down into the cathedral, and from the Golden Gallery outside across the City, the best vantage point to pick out the pinnacles of Wren's parish churches.

The glorious baroque west front of St. Paul's Cathedral, with Queen Victoria's statue in the foreground. (overleaf)

Although only twenty-three of his original fifty-one survive (plus six of his towers), and many of these are dwarfed by tall office blocks, Wren's churches are the most remarkable architectural treasure in the City. Here the full variety, imagination and flair of Wren's genius is most striking. The individuality of design is staggering, varying from the complex domed St. Stephen Walbrook, a miniature predecessor of St. Paul's, to the double-cube simplicity of St. Lawrence Jewry. In some cases, such as St. Vedast, he reproduced the previous medieval plan, or employed orthodox Gothic style as at St. Mary Aldermary with his own version of fan vaulting. In others, Wren imposed a startling Baroque freshness, as in St. Mary Abchurch, St. Bride's Fleet Street and St. Magnus the Martyr, with its sumptuous interior – 'Inexplicable splendour of Ionian white and gold'(T. S. Eliot). No two are the same, similarly decorated or furnished.

Amid such daring originality it is amazing that Wren had the creative energy to design his magnum opus at Greenwich, as well as Chelsea Hospital, Trinity College Library in Cambridge, Tom Tower in Oxford, and Hampton Court. By 1687 the fifty-one churches were finished except for the towers and steeples. These he added last, meticulously designed to complement the dome of St. Paul's and create a new silhouette for the City. Successive Bishops of London greedily sold off twenty-six City churches, nineteen of them Wren's, for redevelopment, and wartime bombing damaged nearly every church. Courageously the majority were repaired or rebuilt although four were lost totally and four more left with only a tower.

Wren's high standards of workmanship rubbed off on others. Forty-four livery company halls were rebuilt, employing many of the craftsmen whom Wren had trained. Edward Strong's elegant gatehouse and James Gibbs' solid quadrangle at St. Bartholomew's Hospital follow in Wren's footsteps, even Hawksmoor's quirky St. Mary Woolnoth, built in 1716. The College of Arms in Queen Victoria Street is the loveliest domestic example of the period, built 1671–1688. The mellow red brick facade, beautifully restored, is protected from the fearsome road traffic by a cobbled courtyard enclosed by the side wings and fabulous wrought-iron gates.

Memories of the Great Fire did not die quickly. Charles II provided £14,000 and asked Wren to design a Monument. Choosing the abandoned site of St. Margaret's Fish Street Hill – the first church destroyed in the Fire – Wren erected a fluted Doric column of Portland stone, capped by an enormous flaming urn. Its height, 202 feet, is the exact distance from the old Pudding Lane bakery. Reliefs around the base depict the heroic exploits of Charles II and his firefighters, while Latin inscriptions blame Popish intriguers. Inside the column, 320 steps lead to a spectacular public viewing platform.

By the time Wren died aged ninety-one in 1723, the City had been reborn. It had entered a new age of prosperity which was to last until 1939, two centuries during which Wren's domes and spires were to dominate the City skyline. There is no national shrine to Christopher Wren, the greatest English architect, only the simple inscription above his tomb in St. Paul's – 'if you seek a memorial, look about you'.

Wren rebuilt St. Vedast off Cheapside on its previous medieval plan but added a startlingly original spire.

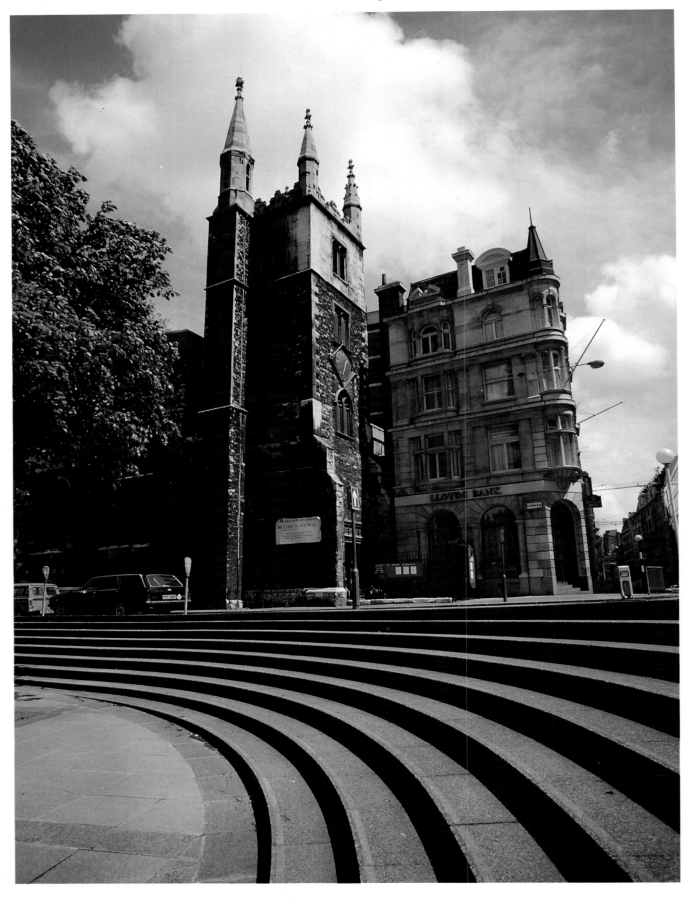

St. Andrew Undershaft, where John Stow is buried, was
one of the few medieval City churches to survive the Fire
and to be untouched by Wren.

8
The Markets

Market places have always been the life-force of the City. As a port, London controlled imports and exports of raw materials and finished products. Markets where goods could be exchanged, prices fixed and orders placed were an integral part of this trading function. They continue to be the most fundamental activity in the City, the corner-stone on which all the other businesses of insurance, shipping, finance, banking and broking rest.

The absence of merchant vessels on the river, the silence of the City wharves and the temporary dereliction of dockland (now changing fast at Wapping and Canary Wharf) make it hard to believe that the Port of London flourished until 1939. Trawlers unloaded fish at Billingsgate even as late as 1947. Although the river still ebbs and flows through its procession of bridges its role as the City's artery has vanished. The main commodity markets have evolved from the handling and sampling of materials to less tangible transactions, appearing on VDUs, print-outs and telex data. Coal, spices, wool and wine have been replaced by share indices, blue chips, international futures, Eurodollars, and exchange rates.

Almost. The exceptions are the ancient wholesale markets run by the City Corporation to supply London's retailers with meat, fish, fruit and vegetables. Sadly, only one survives on its medieval site, Smithfield meat market. Fitz-stephen in 1174 described a

> smooth field where every Friday there is a celebrated rendezvous of fine horses to be sold, swine with their deep flanks, and cows and oxen of immense bulk.

Over the centuries this modest affair expanded, inexorably keeping pace with the growth of London. By 1850 it presented an appalling public health hazard – a nightmare for residents, drovers and the animals, goaded through London's filthy overcrowded streets – benefitting only the City Corporation who collected tolls from the two million livestock sold annually.

Finally a Royal Commission ordered its closure in 1855 together with the squalid butchers' market in Newgate Shambles.

The construction of the world's first underground railway, the Metropolitan Line, inspired the decision to build a new dead meat market at Smithfield. Opened in 1868 on the site of the old pens it was ingeniously located above railway sidings which received freshly-killed meat from all corners of the British Isles. Enormous cold stores with ornate facades were erected to hold refrigerated imports from the colonies.

Smithfield meat market today remains the biggest in Europe and one of London's great characters. Most meat is now home or EEC grown, and arrives in heavy trucks. (The railway sidings closed in 1963 after the Beeching axe and the cold stores fell empty when the docks declined.) Horace Jones's original design, however, is largely unchanged, a masterly blend of function and aesthetics. Elegant open ironwork and louvres provide natural light and ventilation but exclude the sun, keeping meat cool even in summer. The Poultry market was rebuilt after a fire in 1958 in a modern idiom.

Inside the market traditional methods of handling persist. Everything at Smithfield is unloaded, carried into the market, displayed for sale, cut up and carried out again, each job clearly demarcated. Starting at midnight 'pullers-back' drag the carcasses to the tailboards of the lorries; pitchers carry them to the hooks inside, half-running to minimize the strain on their backs (this is the Smithfield shuffle); humpers and shopmen weigh and mark the meat. Trading begins at 5 a.m. and finishes by 8 a.m. Meanwhile cutters skilfully dissect the primary joints, placing the heads, hearts, livers and suet into huge bins for specialist customers. Nothing is wasted. Buyers must employ licensed porters to carry their purchases out of the market, or hire the freelance 'bummarees' who charge per piece carried, cash. Labour costs, not surprisingly, account for 4% of the eventual retail price.

Old hands reckon that Smithfield is a shadow of its former self. Trade has gone to suburban depots and supermarkets. In the 1970s alarmists predicted closure or relocation. Throughput fell from 400,000 tons in 1963 to 233,000 in 1975. It is now more stable, supported by central London butchers and caterers, though many stalls no longer open on Fridays. The City Corporation seem likely to condense operations into the meat and poultry sections, selling off the under-used general markets next to Farringdon Road.

Many of the market-related businesses – sausage makers, bacon curers and offal merchants – have disappeared from the side streets. Architects and ad-men move in to enjoy the dwindling quaintness, helping the process on its way. The City is outwardly committed to keeping Smithfield, but for how long? Savour while you may the barrows piled with meat, the blood-stained coats and the pavements sprinkled with sawdust.

The Corporation's two other major wholesale markets lie outside the City. Spitalfields fruit, vegetable and flower market is just north, between Commercial Street and Bishopsgate, overlooked by Hawksmoor's austere Christchurch spire. Spitalfields, founded in 1682 but acquired and rebuilt by the City from 1893 to 1922 in great hangars, has always bowed to Covent Garden, competing with Borough, Stratford, Greenwich and Western International for second place. Its main advantage, apart from being north of the river, is the proximity of the London Fruit Exchange in Brushfield Street, relocated from Pudding Lane in 1928. Gigantic fruit auctions were held until 1973 but major trade deals are now organized by private treaty. The recent decision to move Spitalfields Market out to Hackney provides colossal opportunities for new development.

Billingsgate fish market, oldest of them all, now occupies a purpose-built warehouse beside West India Dock. Before it moved in January 1982 the market had stood between Lower Thames Street and the river, the same site where fish had been landed, gutted and sold since Saxon times. New Billingsgate, three miles east, is a world away and has shed many long-established customs, though it still works at night, like Smithfield and Spitalfields.

The old market buildings, designed by James Bunning, were saved by a preservation order, their cavernous basements unthawed, the delicate grillwork masking the ghostly emptiness of the trading hall. Traffic could at last speed unfettered along the Lower Thames Street racetrack and developers could play their game of Monopoly on the abandoned lorrypark next door, but the City has lost an old friend. No more on warm summer mornings does the tang of fish waft up from the river on a soft southern breeze through the narrow lanes towards the financial palaces of Lombard Street. Fish Street Hill now evokes only memories, its cobbles no longer slippery with oil and slime. Gone are the shabby 'scats' sitting on broken pallets waiting for work, the frozen breath of the 'stand-boys' leaning on their trolleys, the rumble of iron-rimmed wheels and the curses mumbled from under the black bobbin hats.

Old Leadenhall, once the main wholesale market for game and poultry, boasts only a handful of butchers and fishmongers to supply livery company banquets with exotic meats. The splendid high-Victorian architecture now shelters retail shops and sandwich bars for lunchtime workers. Cheapside, where the medieval costermongers set out their carts and trestles in the middle of the road, is today lined with expensive gentlemen's outfitters, newsagents, camera bazaars and sports equipment boutiques. Far more exciting are the street markets just beyond the City boundary at Leather Lane, Whitecross Street and Wentworth Street. The latter expands on Sundays to become London's most famous street market, Petticoat Lane, choking Middlesex Street with hundreds of stalls, mainly selling clothes. It draws thousands of people, perhaps too many tourists to be London's cheapest, but it is a sight not to be missed. Try Tubby Isaacs' jellied eels, and mind the pick-pockets!

At the opposite end of the scale, dealing in colossal sums of money and vast quantities of produce, are the City's Commodity Markets. The London Commercial Sale Rooms in Mark Lane and Plantation House in Fenchurch Street fix prices and place orders for a wide range of commodities – coffee, rubber, cocoa, sugar, soya and vegetable oil. Deals are struck by 'phone and telex, except for 'futures' (promises to take deliveries in the future) where business is conducted in 'open out-cry' on the trading floor. Futures in grain, like wheat and barley, are auctioned in the Baltic Exchange and the Corn Exchange in Mark Lane, where occasionally samples are exhibited. Only ivory, tea and fur are still regularly sold on the basis of samples. Beaver House in Great Trinity Lane is the headquarters of the historic Hudson Bay Company, founded in 1670. In these auction rooms one-quarter of the world's furs are imported and re-exported, by far the largest international market of its kind.

Leadenhall Market, with its lovely Victorian iron work roof, is the nicest place to shop in the City.

A pitcher carrying sides of beef into Smithfield meat market, the last great wholesale market on its original medieval site.

*The Pearly King of the City of London regularly collects
for charity at the Sunday Petticoat Lane market.*

As pure theatre, the hurly-burly of the 'ring' in the London Metal Exchange or the trading floor of the International Financial Futures Exchange in the Royal Exchange are most spectacular. Amid the shouts, waving of arms and throwing of papers bargains are reached with astonishing rapidity. The quiet dignity of the Gold Market where the price is fixed twice daily by five appointed members is a solemn contrast.

Biggest of all in terms of wealth handled is the Stock Exchange, the money market where stocks and shares worth £1 billion per day are bartered in a complex society of jobbers, brokers, blue-buttons and waiters. These attendants recall the origins of the Stock Exchange – the seventeenth-century Jonathan's coffee house where merchants met to do business, and from where they issued stocks and shares to raise cash from the public to invest in new ventures. Today the Stock Exchange has grown to include 4,500 members, and towering above the trading floor thousands of analysts, advisors and computer technicians sift data and information in brokers' offices. But if you are overawed as you look down from the superb visitors' gallery on to the trading floor where brokers swarm like worker bees around the 'queen' jobbers amid a honeycomb of kiosks, remember that it is only a market place. The Stock Exchange, with its mysterious jargon of 'bulls' and 'bears', gilts, mines and closing prices, is the financial barometer of the economy, and a beacon for dealers in New York, Zurich, Tokyo and Melbourne, but its participants, for all their skill and judgement, are playing a sophisticated game of chance, the risk business.

9
Financial Palaces

Feeding off the City's markets are the industries of banking, insurance, shipping and accountancy. Here the full complexity of the City's financial network is revealed, a myriad of specialist firms and brokers, clustered around the great financial pillars of the Bank of England, Lloyd's, the Baltic Exchange and Stock Exchange.

These activities, initially ancillary to buying and selling, importing and exporting, elevated the City to financial capital of the world, a position maintained despite two world wars and post-war competition from abroad. The value of this success to the economy is prodigious. The City earns annually about £4 billion net in foreign exchange – nearly half Britain's entire 'invisible' income. Without it our balance of payments would be deplorable. The City's expertise undoubtedly promotes British exports and is crucial in financing Governmental and private investment. It holds, practically if not politically, the purse strings.

The idea of banking, rather than hiding money under the mattress, came with the Lombards. Many pecuniary terms have come from Italy, notably £.s.d. (librae, solidi, denarii). The Goldsmiths rented safe deposits in their vaults, and the Royal Mint was also established as a bank. These funds, however, were frequently raided by the king, as by Charles I in 1640. Five years after the Convention in 1689 Parliament welcomed William Paterson's scheme for a new bank which protected individual savings from the Crown and raised funds centrally for the Government at fixed interest rates. The Bank of England was born. Its first loan was for the Dutch wars; as the Government's bank it rapidly became the bankers' bank.

Lying in the heart of the City the Bank occupies a three acre street block, once a parish on its own. The inner courtyard, with trees and fountain, is all that remains of St. Christopher-le-Stocks and its graveyard. In 1788 impressive new buildings were erected by Sir John Soane. The interior was gutted and rebuilt by Herbert

Baker in 1921, keeping Soane's impregnable rusticated outer wall, devoid of windows. The Bank of England pioneered banking practice and respectability. Sheridan's affectionate description in 1797 of 'an elderly lady in the City of great credit and understanding' stuck: the Bank is still nicknamed the Old Lady of Threadneedle Street. Sartorial traditions survive; the chief gatekeeper flaunts an emblazoned gown, two-cornered hat and tall staff. The porters sport scarlet waistcoats, pink tails and gold-trimmed top hats, like outrageous flunkies.

By 1833 the Bank had a virtual monopoly in issuing banknotes and became the central clearing house for other banks. Nationalisation in 1946 cemented its pivotal role in supervising the financial welfare of the country. Its vaults store the Government's gold and its 5,000 employees monitor the affairs of the money market and other nations, ready to rescue emergencies. The magic figures, M0 and M3, are calculated and fed to the Treasury. Its power and responsibilities are enormous.

Merchant banking originated in the eighteenth century around expanding commodity markets, raising cash for merchant venturers. Many were founded by immigrants – Hambro, Lazard, Schroder, Warburg and, most famous, Rothschild. This century has seen a flood of foreign banks. The Moscow Narodny Bank arrived in 1919, followed by American, Japanese, Arabian and European equivalents, originally seeking to serve their compatriots' business interests in Britain. Over 500 foreign banks are now represented, and increasingly they are forming consortiums and international syndicates to pursue joint ventures. Their presence ensures the City's banking supremacy.

Many financial institutions in the City began in the fashionable seventeenth-century coffee

The Bank of England, or 'The Old Lady of Threadneedle Street', supervises the financial welfare of the City and the nation. (overleaf)

houses. Here merchants and brokers could deal and exchange bills and cheques in comfort and some confidentiality. The Baltic Coffee House organised movements of ships in the Baltic Sea. Today 75% of the world's bulk cargo is negotiated by the 2,500 members of the Baltic Exchange in St. Mary Axe. Tankers are marshalled worldwide to carry the great staples – coal, grain, iron-ore, oil and bauxite. Air chartering is a growing side-shoot.

Insurance was virtually unknown before 1666. Fire insurance offices sprang up soon after, employing their own firemen and labelling their clients' buildings with special firemarks a few of which can still be seen. In 1688 brokers operating from Edward Lloyd's humble coffee houses, first in Tower Street and then in Lombard Street, instigated marine insurance. Lloyd himself encouraged business by publishing shipping news, but could never have envisaged the scale of Richard Rogers' shiny wonderland in Lime Street. The famous Lutine Bell (captured from a French frigate) is still rung, once for bad news, twice for good, but Lloyd's today underwrite almost anything, not just ships. Its 19,000 syndicated members bear all losses. Lloyd's is the epitome of security.

Until 1925 Lloyd's used the Royal Exchange, rebuilt after 1666 but destroyed again by fire in 1838. The musical clock chimed 'There's Nae Luck Aboot the Hoose' as it burnt down! William Tite's replacement with its Corinthian columns provides an imposing foil to the Mansion House and Bank of England. Since September 1982 it has housed the London Inter-

national Financial Futures Exchange which speculates in future interest rates. The Chicago equivalent hires American footballers to reserve the best dealing positions. While not so physically rough, LIFFE has much of that noisy razzmatazz – note the dealers' pyjama-blazers!

The City has adapted faster than anywhere to the opportunities of new markets and financial services. Gone are the fusty leather-bound ledgers, crusty clerks and steep rickety stairs. Today the City buzzes with snappily besuited men and trimly dressed women. Behind grey-tinted glass, open-plan offices hum with terminals and processors; plush marble foyers sprout tropical plants on seas of deep-pile carpet. Foresight, flexibility and speed are crucial to the City's continuing domination of world finance. Behind this lie the fundamental principles of trust and mutual confidence. 'My word is my bond' is the Stock Exchange's motto; 'Fidentia' is Lloyd's. It applies throughout; a verbal agreement is tantamount to a binding contract. This is the secret of the City's success, in a world where a nod of the head or a shake of the hand can be worth millions of pounds.

At a time of increasing competition from financial markets elsewhere in the world and rival ventures in Dockland, the City's reputation for integrity and adaptability has never before been so scrutinised. Over the centuries the City has always answered its critics and adversaries in the best possible manner, and will surely continue to do so.

The high-tech image of Mondial House contrasts with the Victorian portal to Cannon Street Station behind.

10
Corporation and Mayor

Many of the cherished traditions and characteristics of the City stem from its unique system of government. The City Corporation oversees the square mile with a liberal democracy stretching back a thousand years. The City prizes its autonomy, the envy of every other local authority in Britain.

After the Roman evacuation London was abandoned as a centre of military power, government and court life. When Saxon settlers and traders reoccupied the City they were left largely to their own devices. At the hustings of the folkmoot the citizens elected thegns to administer justice and chose elders or aldermen from their own ranks to represent the interests of each district or ward. The City evolved a rare degree of self-government, almost like the city states of Europe where national unity and defence developed painfully slowly.

Through its growing economic clout the City claimed the right to 'approve' the king. When Canute left no natural heir the City elected Edward the Confessor. William the Conqueror removed their say but signed a charter with the City fathers pledging to retain their laws in return for their allegiance. Much of this independence survives. Rights and privileges negotiated over the centuries from monarchs and governments have been jealously guarded. Wise investment of the City's wealth through the acquisition of freedoms and concessions has ensured the City's continuing power base.

In Saxon times the City's leading spokesman was the Portreeve (literally in charge of the port, just as a sheriff controlled a shire). In 1191 this office was elevated to the title of mayor and bestowed on Henry Fitzaylwin. In the same year King John, heavily in debt to City coffers, agreed to the Commune of London. Just before the Magna Carta in 1215 John signed a special charter allowing the annual election of a new mayor, to be 'faithful, discreet and fit for the government of the City'. He was supported by two sheriffs and the aldermen. About one-third of adult males could vote – freemen and their sons and 'qualified' craftsmen in a trade. The links between the guilds and elected officers were cemented: power became concentrated in the hands of wealthy merchants and liverymen.

Records of decisions, regulations and procedures have been carefully kept since 1275. Edward I approved the forming of the City's Common Council in 1295, based on his Model Parliament. It has governed the City ever since. The Common Council comprises the Court of Aldermen (rather like Parliament's House of Lords) and the 'commoners', elected by the twenty-five wards to supervise the common affairs of the City. Commoners must seek re-election; aldermen, who must be liverymen, serve for life, or until the age of seventy. Two factors distinguish the City. The immense business vote far outweighs the residents' in most wards, guaranteeing that livery companies are strongly represented. Second, the absence of party political affiliations frees debate from dogmatic party lines and whips. Decisions are taken on their merits, always to advance the welfare and status of the City.

The Court of Common Council meets in the Guildhall. This great hall dates from 1411, twice burnt down in 1666 and 1940 and twice rebuilt. Behind the Gothic porch and pinnacles, added by George Dance, the medieval walls and crypt survive. Beneath the magnificent timber roof the two giants, Gog and Magog, glare down from the gallery. Statues of great statesmen look on more benignly from the sides. Outside, the wide courtyard has been enclosed by forthright new civic buildings, the white concrete yet to blend with the mellow stone of Guildhall and St. Lawrence Jewry.

The City Corporation performs statutory duties like any other local authority – street cleaning, rubbish collection, environmental health, libraries, and mending roads. Although nine-tenths of rate receipts are lost under the rate equalisation scheme the basic municipal services are of the highest standard. Note the rarity of lamp-posts – street lights are attached to

The Guildhall, centre of the City's government, and the most famous town hall in England.

buildings. In addition the Corporation has responsibilities which pre-date official local government. The Chamberlain (director of finance) handles not only the £350 million annual rate income but also manages two ancient private funds, the Bridge House Estates and the City Cash. The Corporation owns one-quarter of the City, freehold; rents total £15 million each year.

In the nineteenth century the City's enormous wealth fostered many admirable social and philanthropic deeds, in keeping with the Corporation's motto, *Domine dirige nos*. The statutory closure of overcrowded city graveyards in 1851 prompted the acquisition of 176 acres of Aldersbrook Farm, Wanstead for a new cemetery. This enabled the conversion of the tiny City churchyards into public gardens. More significantly the Wanstead cemetery conferred commoners' rights on the Corporation for Epping Forest which was under threat from felling, enclosure and re-development. The Corporation vigorously supported the conservation lobby, won the court battle and in 1878 bought 5,600 acres of Epping Forest for the recreational benefit of Londoners. Over the next twenty years Burnham Beeches in Buckinghamshire, West Ham Park, Highgate Wood, Queen's Park in

Kilburn and Coulsdon Common were acquired – 7,000 acres of public open space, ten times bigger than the City itself.

The Corporation built housing estates and old peoples' homes in adjoining boroughs, still immaculately maintained. They also own and fund the wholesale markets, the Guildhall Museum and Art Gallery, the Barbican Centre and the Guildhall School of Music and Drama, all beyond normal duties. As Port of London Health Authority the Corporation controls twenty miles of river, and even runs an animal quarantine station at Heathrow Airport.

The most feted and colourful figure in City government is the Lord Mayor. This is the pinnacle, the highest accolade any man or woman can receive. It is the essence of the legendary Dick Whittington, mayor four times, in 1397, 1398, 1406, 1419. His vast wealth came partly from coal whose import tax had been waived by Henry V to repay the City loans which financed his Agincourt army. Coal barges were called 'cats', hence perhaps the derivation of Whittington's mythically lucky feline friend!

A Lord Mayor must first be a liveryman and alderman, and serve as either Lay or Aldermanic Sheriff. The mayor is elected on Michaelmas Day in the Guildhall by the assembly of liverymen, wearing their full regalia. In practice the choice for the next few years is predictable; rarely is the line of succession broken. Six weeks later, on the second Friday of November the outgoing mayor bows to the new, in the moving Silent Ceremony. The following day, Lord Mayor's Day, is a noisy festive contrast, highlighted by the Lord Mayor's Show. This procession embarks from Guildhall, passing Cheapside, St. Paul's, Ludgate Circus and Fleet Street en route to the Strand, returning along the Embankment and Queen Victoria Street to Mansion House. On the way the new mayor is identified to the City, and at the Royal Courts of Justice he or she is accepted on behalf of the monarch by the Lord Chief Justice and judges of the Queen's Bench, as decreed by King John's charter.

The Show was introduced in 1454 by Mayor Norman. For 200 years it was a waterborne carnival from Queenshithe to Westminster, the decorated barges decked out with bands and entertainers – hence the word 'float'. Since 1757 the Mayor has ridden in the beautifully gilded coach, displayed for the rest of the year in the Museum of London. This gleaming four-ton marvel is pulled by six mighty dray horses from Whitbread's brewery and escorted by the musketeers, pikemen and drummers of the Honourable Artillery Company, the nation's oldest regiment. Everybody joins in the fun. The mayor doffs the famous tricorn hat and waves the black and gold robes to the cheerful crowds lining the pavements. It remains one of London's great pageants, a spectacle to rival Trooping the Colour. It comes at a special time of year, as London inhales the last breath of autumn, chilly November air misty with the acrid haze of bonfire night, the stubborn leaves clinging to their summer branches, loth to join their fallen comrades on Remembrance Sunday. The City streets are swept clean – out with the old and in with the new.

The Lord Mayor is invariably a worthy and respected person. Traditionally each adopts a particular charity for fund-raising during the year of office. In the last century the first Jewish and Catholic mayors were elected. In 1983 Lady Donaldson became the first lady Lord Mayor. Mansion House is the Lord Mayor's official residence. Built in 1739 its grand exterior hides a sumptuous interior, rich with elaborate plasterwork and opulent State Rooms. A posse of footmen, butlers and housemaids ensure a lifestyle of luxurious comfort. This palatial splendour is some compensation for the hard-work of mayoralty. The Lord Mayor's banquet where the Prime Minister and hundreds of illustrious guests sit alongside 400 yards of table cloth, is one of hundreds of dinners and functions which must be attended and speeches delivered. The Corporation's Remembrancer assists with day-to-day organisation but cannot supply the energy, enthusiasm and dignity which the mayor must exude.

Strange customs such as the Quit Rents ceremony, when the City Comptroller hands a horseshoe and nails to the Queen's Remembrancer as 'rent' for Crown land in the City, are, like the Lord Mayor's Show, funded out of ancient City coffers, not out of the rates. The City fathers, cunningly protecting their wealth from state and monarch, have generously and shrewdly honoured their heroes in style, from Henry V's triumphant march-past to the Falklands' Victory Parade in October 1982. On that grey day three-quarters of a million people crammed the City streets and balconies, pigeons flew in wild alarm as Vulcan bombers and Harrier jump-jets roared above the City skyline, and 1,200 servicemen enjoyed a champagne luncheon in the Guildhall. It was £23,000 well spent out of the Lord Mayor's fund.

The City has also hosted some of the finest State occasions – Queen Victoria's diamond jubilee service in St. Paul's Cathedral, Winston Churchill's solemn funeral cortège, and the joyous Royal Wedding of Charles and Diana. These ceremonies and celebrations provide a soothing antidote to the cut and thrust of City business life, and infuse an irreplaceable flavour into the English calendar. Like many of the things we take for granted, they would be sorely missed.

The Lord Mayor in his coach, acquainting himself with his citizens during the Lord Mayor's Show.

11
Law and Order

The complex business world of buying and selling, banking and insurance, is not the only aspect of the City's working life. The bastions of law and order are equally famous institutions in the City, fulfilling vital functions in the administration of justice and the unceasing litigation of commercial wrangles.

Since 1839 the City Corporation has run its own special police force, separate from the Metropolitan Police and, uniquely, outside the direct jurisdiction of the Home Office. The force of 1,300 men and women is distinguished by height (five feet eleven inches minimum) and splendid Roman-style helmets, gold braid and buttons. The modern headquarters in Wood Street is coincidentally near the site of the early Roman garrison at the Barbican. In many ways the City Police are a natural descendant of the local militia, far more of a presence in the daily life of the City than the old City regiment, the Honourable Artillery Company, which is actually based outside the City near Bunhill Fields.

In medieval times the nightwatchmen and constables struggled to stem the theft and violence which proliferated on the City streets despite curfews and savage punishments. A baker caught selling underweight loaves would be pilloried; the penalty for stealing bread was death. Today the City Police are an elite, well-paid unit, noted for efficiency and courtesy. Their duties include patrolling the forty-eight miles of City streets, undertaking the onerous task of maintaining public order and protecting royalty and VIP's on their frequent visits to the City. The Mounted Branch are renowned for their superbly disciplined grey horses, often seen exercising in the streets. Special squads look after the Corporation's wholesale markets where traffic control, pilfering and petty crimes are a niggling problem. Highly-trained sections deal exclusively with fraud enquiries and business irregularities, arguably the most important aspect of law and order in the City today, when a reputation for honesty and trustworthiness is so crucial to its future.

The dispensing of justice for 'domestic' City affairs is handled at the Mayor's and City of London Court, which is the County Court for the City. In these two courtrooms, next door to the Guildhall in Gresham Street, circuit judges adjudicate on civil disputes and claims. Minor criminal matters are dealt with at the magistrates' courts within the Guildhall and the Mansion House. The Lord Mayor is the City's Chief Magistrate on the bench of aldermen. The ornate Justice Room in Mansion House remains the only courtroom in Britain in a private house.

Standing on the site of the notorious Newgate prison, the Central Criminal Court is the country's most famous legal establishment, better known as the Old Bailey, though this is really the name of the narrow side street outside. The Old Bailey is the 'High Court' of the criminal world, but maintained at the City Corporation's expense, to the relief of the taxpayer.

From the early 1200s Newgate, with its massive iron-fettered gates, was used by the Corporation to intern the most dangerous felons and robbers. Minor lock-ups and gaols, such as the Fleet Prison, Giltspur and London Bridge compters, housed lesser criminals and debtors. Traitors and political opponents went to the Tower, and rarely left. Conditions in Newgate deteriorated appallingly in the eighteenth century. Chronic overcrowding and abysmal sanitation contaminated the water and fuelled epidemics. Food and favours had to be bought from corrupt turnkeys. Judges in the Old Bailey, built next to the prison in 1539, wore nosegays of sweet-smelling herbs to ward off the foul odours, although they proved ineffective against gaol fever. The tradition is still carried on at the opening of sessions.

Many famous people 'did time' at Newgate. Ben Jonson, Christopher Marlowe and Daniel Defoe were fortunate to survive the experience. Troublemakers were flogged at the barbaric whipping post, now displayed in the Museum of London. Those condemned to death were taken to Tyburn gallows (near Marble Arch). At the start of the long bumpy journey the open

The outstretched arms of Justice hold the sword and scales high above the dome of the Central Criminal Court, better known as the Old Bailey.

cart stopped outside St. Sepulchre's where the great bell was rung; 'when will you pay me, say the bells of Old Bailey'. After the prison was rebuilt in 1770 executions were transferred to the prison yard, attracting riotous crowds of ghoulish spectators. Michael Barret was the last to be hanged publicly, in 1868. The severity of Victorian justice could not mask the intolerable squalor within. Convicted and unconvicted alike shared dingy, damp dungeons with rats and lice. 'Those dreadful walls of Newgate which have hidden so much misery and such unspeakable anguish,' wrote Dickens.

New model penitentiaries like Pentonville and Wormwood Scrubs enabled the demolition of Newgate in 1902. In its place Edward Mountford's fine neo-baroque court rooms were completed by 1907. The elegant dome is surmounted by the familiar golden figure of Justice, twelve feet high, sword and scales outstretched, but her face unblindfolded, to show that here, at least, Justice is not blind. Behind the boldly rusticated stone walls the twenty-three courts hear the nation's most serious criminal cases. No. I Court is the showcase where the great dramas of criminal justice have unfolded, from the trial of

Dr. Crippen in 1910 to the Yorkshire Ripper in 1981. 'Protect the Children of the Poor and Punish the Wrongdoer' is appropriately inscribed above the entrance. Eight times a year the Lord Mayor presides in court, and in his absence a central seat is always left empty, backed by the Sword of Office.

The Lord Mayor's absolute authority in the Old Bailey contrasts with the independence of the Inner and Middle Temples. Ever since the Knights of St. John inherited the confiscated property of the papist Knights Templar and leased the land between Fleet Street and the river to groups of law students in the fourteenth century this has been a haven for lawyers. In 1608 James I perpetuated their right to conduct their affairs without interference, putting them on a par with Lincoln's Inn and Gray's Inn outside the City. The round Norman Temple church survives within a network of courtyards and passages. In this old-fashioned world barristers nurture their Oxbridge roots. Dinners in hall and academic staircases summon their pupils to the bar. Names of members of chambers are neatly lettered, black on cream, in the doorways of quaintly-named terraces – Crown Office Row and Paper Buildings. Of the 500 chambers one-quarter are residential, though under pressure to change. In the quads shadows and footsteps flit across the echoing slabs. Studious lodgings

look out over walks and lawns, sundials and fountains. In the rose gardens Yorkists and Lancastrians picked their red and white emblems. Among the venerable trees this peaceful enclave remains a retreat from the noisy reality of the world outside.

'Protect the Children of the Poor and Punish the Wrongdoer' is inscribed above the entrance of the Old Bailey – severe but reassuring.

12
Imperial Splendour

The prosperity of Victorian and Edwardian Britain wrought enormous social and physical change on the City. Between 1841 and 1914 the City's population fell from 123,000 to about 15,000. Residents left in droves; new roads, railways and commercial buildings altered the whole character of the City.

Since medieval times, richer merchants escaped from the City's smells and pestilence to country retreats, such as Thomas Gresham's Osterley. Increasingly, successful exponents of Victorian entrepreneurial endeavour coupled their business acumen with aristocratic domesticity. Nathan Rothschild, grandest of nineteenth-century bankers, lived in style at Gunnersbury. The arrival of railways revolutionised transport. Quick, cheap travel released even the humblest clerks and shopkeepers from living above their workplace. Spacious suburbs with trees and fresh air proved immediately attractive.

Railway termini at Liverpool Street, Fenchurch Street, Cannon Street, Broad Street (demolished) and Holborn Viaduct cleared away acres of slums and became new City magnets. In 1863 the Metropolitan Line linked other main-line stations to Farringdon Street and Moorgate, cut and covered beside the culverted Fleet River. It paved the way for London's underground, providing faster, cleaner transport into the heart of the City. Tube stations mushroomed, the Bank's in the vestibule of St. Mary Woolnoth!

The Victorians had supreme confidence in their engineering skills. A strong national belief in 'progress' removed all obstacles to change. Sir Joseph Bazalgette masterminded London's new drainage system and the Victoria, Albert and Chelsea Embankments. This most adventurous undertaking narrowed the river, creating wide boulevards and gardens over colossal outfall sewers. New roads radically improved travel above ground. King William Street in 1835 set a trend for bold diagonals, bypassing old bottle-necks. Holborn Viaduct, opened by Queen Victoria in 1869, linked Newgate Street with Holborn, spanning the Fleet valley on ornate cast-iron bridges, 400 yards long. 4,000 homes were demolished. Queen Victoria Street (1870), Throgmorton Avenue (1875) and Lloyd's Avenue (1899) swept away the ancient lanes of Bucklersbury, Austin and Crutched Friars.

Flanking such impressive streets, imposing offices and salerooms were erected in stone, brick and terracotta. Architectural fashion embraced lavish Italianate and Venetian styles, Flemish gables and Palladian classicism. Excessive fairy-tale castles, like Waterhouse's Prudential Building, covered whole street blocks. Triangular corners inspired assertive curves and turrets, or fantasies like the art nouveau Black Friar tavern. The wholesale markets were pompously rebuilt between 1848 and 1881. Fishmongers and other livery companies enlarged and enriched their halls. The Victorians even embellished medieval and Wren churches with ugly glass and insensitive pinnacles.

1900 was the zenith of British imperial splendour, epitomised by Lutyens House in Finsbury Square and Edwin Cooper's PLA Building (now Amalgamated House) in Trinity House Square. Trams rattled through the streets. Shoe-shine boys, flower girls and road sweepers flocked the pavements. Clerks from Holloway and Camberwell scurried to daily drudgery with the 'dead sound on the final stroke of nine'. Nothing, it seemed, could harm the magnificent ascendance of the City, proudly heading the world's largest empire. Few could foresee the calamity of war.

The Royal Exchange, rebuilt in 1838 by William Tite, looks with its grandiose facade towards the Mansion House and Bank of England.

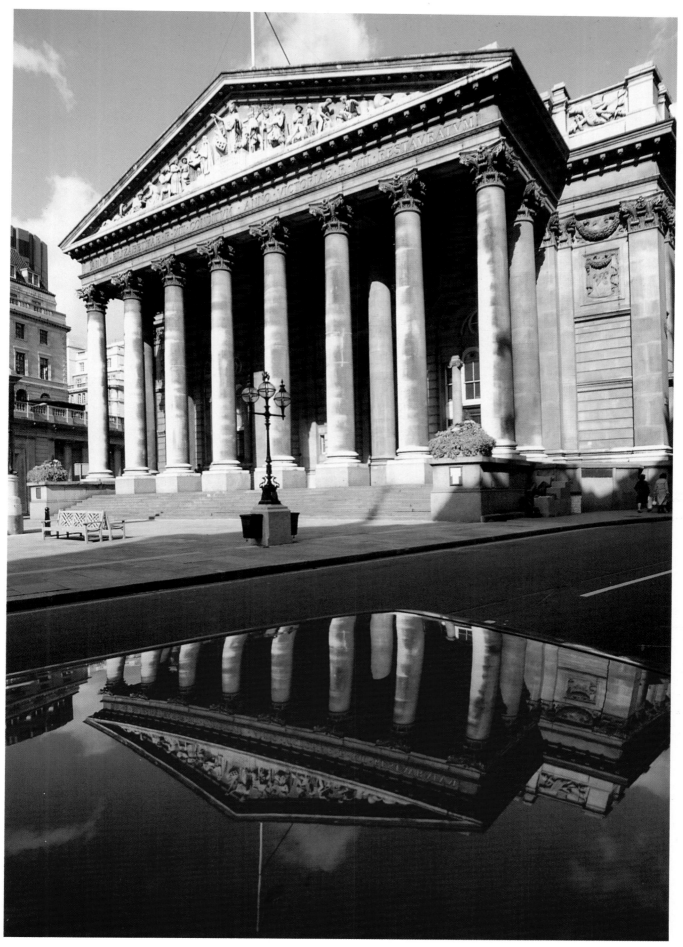

*A reminder of imperial wealth and splendour, embossed
on the side of Plantation House, Fenchurch Street.*

13
The Second Fire

At the outbreak of the Second World War in September 1939 everyone dreaded mass gas attacks on London. Few suspected that the main threat to the City would be that age-old destroyer, fire. Yet, in December 1940 as much damage was caused on one night as had taken several days in 1666.

Outraged by daring RAF raids on Berlin and encouraged by successful incendiary attacks on Coventry and Manchester, Göring and his henchman General Feldmarschall Sperrle, commander of Luftflotte 3 in northern France, plotted their revenge. On the Sunday between Christmas and New Year the City of London was deserted, its buildings locked and their owners away for the holiday. A few faithful fire-spotters stood duty. That night an abnormally low tide in the North Sea drained the Thames to little more than a trickle. Low cloud provided perfect cover for German bombers, rendering RAF night-fighters impotent. Anti-aircraft guns were noisy but ineffective, mainly boosting civilian morale.

Guided by their infamous X-beams the first German pathfinder arrived over St. Paul's at 6.08 p.m., and released five molotov bread-baskets, each of which showered thirty-six magnesium incendiary bombs, to be followed over the next five hours by another 140 Heinkel and Junker bombers. On impact each incendiary burnt white hot for ten minutes, like a large incandescent sparkler. Of the 24,000 dropped, hundreds fell into the river, others clattered onto streets or concrete where they fizzled harmlessly. Some were dowsed by fire-watchers with sandbags and wet sacks, but many hit unattended roof-tops where they burnt through lead and pitch starting dozens of fires.

Within half-an-hour fires were raging all over the City and a dim red blush lit the way for incoming German pilots. The five City fire-stations were inundated with SOS calls, but by 7.30 every fire engine in the whole of Greater London was in action. Aldersgate Street and Redcross Street fire stations were themselves both uncontrollably ablaze. The fire brigades' efforts were hampered by a dire water shortage. With water-mains into the City broken by bombs, pressure fell to zero. Fireboats on the Thames were out of range; the mud banks proved too wide to drag hosepipes. Collapsing buildings began to block streets. Stranded fire appliances were abandoned as their tyres melted in the mounting heat.

The City's Victorian and Edwardian buildings were highly combustible, full of timber, and often crowded closely together among narrow streets and alleys. North of St. Paul's the Paternoster Row area was crammed with the six million books of publishing companies and warehouses packed with textiles. Individual fires rapidly spread and coalesced into an unquenchable inferno, an embryonic fire-storm – a hideous phenomenon which later in the war destroyed Hamburg and Dresden in Allied attacks. A huge pillar of flame cut through the clouds, visible from Bishops Stortford and Isleworth, and to airborne German pilots from the French coast, like a giant beacon. Flying at 16,000 feet their planes were buffeted by the turbulent hot updrafts.

St. Paul's, illuminated by the surrounding blaze, was hit by hundreds of incendiaries and smothered with sparks. The roof of the choir became dangerously hot, and one excitable American journalist prematurely reported that the cathedral was alight. One bomb did lodge in the lead dome, but fell through harmlessly. The watch magnificently stood their ground; miraculously St. Paul's was saved. Elsewhere fire-fighters were hopelessly outnumbered. The Central Telephone Exchange in Wood Street burnt down without a bucket of water thrown on it. St. Lawrence Jewry, barred and bolted, blazed unchecked. Its flaming steeple collapsed, showering the adjacent Guildhall roof with embers which soon took hold. Historic records and manuscripts were hastily rescued from the vaults.

The last bomb fell at 11.30. A second attack by

The dome of St. Paul's miraculously escaped destruction
in the Blitz and became a symbol of London's defiance
against German bombing.

The wedding-cake steeple of St. Bride's, happily restored
47 years after it burnt like a torch in the Second Fire.

160 bombers, dropping high explosives into the fire-storm, was cancelled owing to the deteriorating weather which turned the French airfields into quagmires. This alone spared the City from total annihilation. Nevertheless, by next morning as workers struggled to find their offices among rubble-strewn streets, the damage was plain. Seventeen churches, thirteen by Wren, were destroyed, including St. Bride's Fleet Street, St. Giles' Cripplegate and St. Stephen's Coleman Street. Only eight were later rebuilt. The fallen stones of St. Mary Aldermanbury were sold to America; the ruins of Christchurch Newgate remain.

Huge areas were totally burnt out – from Chancery Lane to Farringdon Street, Newgate to Blackfriars, Aldersgate to Moorgate and from Cheapside to Old Street. At Moorgate station the heat had melted glass and buckled railway tracks. In the east, hundreds of buildings had disappeared between Fenchurch Street and Lower Thames Street, from Houndsditch to Minories. Countless documents, deeds and contracts were incinerated inside safes. Only a small enclave around the Bank of England was unscathed. One and a half square miles of the City and its immediate neighbourhood were laid waste.

Within the City surprisingly few people were killed. Twelve firemen perished under falling masonry, 123 others were injured. North of the City boundary scores more died, trapped in tenement blocks and basements. Repairs to road and rail took weeks. Many damaged buildings had to be pulled down. Although Lloyd's resumed 'business as usual' in its sixty-feet deep shelter, numerous City firms were ruined, their employees paid off.

The City continued to suffer spasmodic bombing until the very end of the war. In May 1941 Bank Station received a direct hit, killing many helpless shelterers. On 8th March 1945, at 11.10 a.m., one of the last V-2 rockets landed catastrophically at the junction of Farringdon Road and Charterhouse Street beside Smithfield Market. 473 people were killed and injured, including a man hit by a flying railway sleeper half a mile away on Blackfriars Bridge. Fortunately it was the only V-2 to strike the City, already so badly scarred and charred from 1940.

Avant-garde architects and planners welcomed the chance to reconstruct the City. Even though some of Wren's finest churches had been irreparably damaged many dreary Victorian buildings had gone as well. 'The Hun is giving us a priceless opportunity to re-conceive the City on a more rational and liveable plan' wrote McDonald Hastings. Paternoster Square, Golden Lane, London Wall and, above all, the Barbican, were to rise like the phoenix from the ashes.

Still falls the Rain –
Dark as the world of man, black as our loss –
Blind as the nineteen hundred and forty nails
Upon the Cross.
(Edith Sitwell)

14
Phoenix Barbican

It takes only one visit to see why the Barbican has been the most controversial post-war development in the City, if not all London. The sheer scale of the buildings, an angular colossus of concrete, steel and brick, swamps the human form awesomely or awfully, according to semantics. Strategically it remains a brilliantly conceived idea which future generations will applaud; its physical realisation, however, is very much 'of its time', flawed and miscalculated.

Reconstruction of the bomb-ravaged City germinated with William Holford's 1947 City of London Plan. This proposed a new precinct (Paternoster Square) immediately north of St. Paul's, and a northern bypass, Route Eleven (London Wall), to be flanked by plain rectangular glass office blocks. 'It promises to be of high aesthetic value and London's most advanced concept of central area development', wrote Nikolaus Pevsner, somewhat naively. North of London Wall sixty acres lay flattened and abandoned, once a maze of little streets. In 1955, fifteen years after its devastation, Duncan Sandys, Minister of Housing and Local Government, proposed this wasteland to spearhead a fresh injection of housing into the City. The Corporation enthusiastically backed the scheme; the Barbican was born.

Chamberlain, Powell and Bon were appointed architects, a young partnership rapt with the theoretical notions of Le Corbusier and the latest fads of the day. High density flats, to hold 6,000 new residents, mainly couples and single people, with a few families housed in maisonettes nearer the ground, was the basis, grouped into massive eight-storey slabs set in squares on a raised podium. Three towers relieve this monotony, thin, triangular, almost graceful, soaring 412 feet above the City, the highest residential buildings in Britain. Concentrated vertical living achieved a big increase in population and the opportunity to provide large amounts of open space and other facilities. What sets the Barbican apart from countless other high-rise redevelopments in post-war London is

its boldness and comprehensiveness. The Barbican is almost a city within the City. New shops, pubs and restaurants, a public library, and new homes for the City of London Girls School, Guildhall School of Music and Drama and the Museum of London (not to be missed) were deliberately included to bring life and purpose to the place.

Such laudable vitality has to compete with an architectural style which is aggressively Brobdingnagian. Gigantic circular columns, of Roman grandeur, prop up the towering superstructure. Vast expanses of smooth brick paving create a harshness which dazzles the eyes in midsummer sun and cows the timid spirit in February gloom. Semi-circular hoods to the long residential blocks and curved edges to balconies and walkways, like clumsy dinner plates, unify but oppress. Sections of Roman wall and barbican have been carefully preserved but are frustratingly unapproachable, frequently isolated by moats or locked gates. Nothing encourages casual wandering. At every corner the pedestrian must reassess orientation, consult a cartographic riddle or follow a bemusing coloured trail. The gutted church of St. Giles Cripplegate was meticulously renovated as a special centrepiece, but is too self-consciously exhibited on a lavatorial pediment where tombstones have been irreverently and vulgarly clumped like building bricks.

The very heart of the Barbican was reserved for an arts and conference centre which after traumatic delays finally opened in 1982. Its design is the saving grace of the Barbican. Within its five acres a staggering variety of functions are squeezed into a multitude of levels, far too clever for immediate comprehension. The lowest cinema, five floors down from the street entrance, lies below sea level. The main theatre where none of the 1,160 seats are more than sixty-five feet from the stage has a flytower 109 feet high. Surrounding this, nine storeys up, the roof garden is a luxuriant wonderland where banana trees and giant cacti flourish in only eighteen inches of soil, requiring daily feeding of

One of the three 412-feet high Barbican Towers, the highest residential buildings in Britain, with the Crescent below.

nutrients (the roof structure can hold only 1,000 tons of soil). Sprawling foyers, rather like plush airport departure lounges, convey an atmosphere of opulence, beneath the glittering cuboid chandelier. Money has not been spared. The arts centre, originally budgetted at £18 million, eventually cost £150 million. The conservatory alone took £1 million and costs £70,000 per annum to run.

The argumentative furore over the arts centre has latterly overshadowed evaluation of the rest of the Barbican. The housing, estimated at £17 million, in the end took £70 million to build. By 1975 maintenance was devouring a subsidy of £4 million each year from City rates. Since then the Corporation has sold off an increasing number of Barbican flats, recouping some capital but losing control over occupancy and scuppering the chance of fostering a close-knit local community. Expensive short-term business penthouses and guest suites do not create a diversified residential population. The dreams of 1955 have not been fulfilled. Perhaps 6,000 residents were never enough on their own without a hefty influx of outsiders. The arts centre with capacity for 4,000 people in its halls has done most to sustain and revitalise local shops, pubs and cafés.

The lake, trees and stone walls of St. Giles' Cripplegate help to soften the 'Brave New World' of the Barbican.

The elevated walkway, segregating pedestrians from cars, was a model planned to cover the whole City. Parking and traffic is tucked beneath the podium, unpleasantly for those who prefer to keep their feet on the ground or who brave Beech Street to find the tube. The elevated promenades and landscaped terraces rarely reward the climb from terra firma. Large trees are difficult to grow in planting tubs. Green grass is limited and largely private to the residents and girls' school, inaccessible to the general public. The elaborate lake with its slick waterfalls and jets is pretty but essentially sterile. It can never match the ceaseless ebb and flow of the river at the South Bank. As an inevitably contrived environment the Barbican feels hard and cold, with a rigidity which will be difficult to soften.

Just as the drab blocks of London Wall and the insensitive Holford slabs next to St. Paul's are now generally accepted as outmoded and undesirable, so the tiresome and inflexible features of the Barbican may increasingly irritate our sensibilities. How will it stand the test of time? Perhaps that should not worry us too much. The tall towers and arts centre have changed the physical and cultural shape of London. It is a new focus for the metropolis. The ponds have even attracted herons to plunder their fish! The Barbican has adventurously and determinedly made its mark; it is impossible to imagine the City without it.

15
The Artistic City

The emergence of a new focus for London's arts over the last twenty years has brought a welcome human face to the City. Traditionally frivolous or insalubrious entertainment had been relegated to suburban venues, like the Globe and Fortune theatres at Southwark and White-cross Street. Travelling players performed at fairs beyond the City's jurisdiction. Courtlife at Westminster and the concentration of nobility and gentry in fashionable Mayfair favoured the West End for cultural innovations. Eighteenth-century pleasure gardens and opera houses became the haunts of high society. The Albert, Queen's and Festival Halls continued to isolate the City from 1851 to the Festival of Britain in 1951.

The City Corporation had, however, founded the Guildhall School of Music and Drama in 1880 and provided grandiose reverberant premises in John Carpenter Street. In 1977 this famous conservatoire transferred to the Barbican. The old Guildhall remains boarded up and silent. Tallis Street, which once echoed with warbling sopranos, exercising cellos and burbling bassoons, has lost its musical associations. Few of the 2,000 students and staff mourned the move into purpose-built accommodation.

The revival of the performing arts in the City began when Bernard Miles and 'other poor players of London' leased and converted derelict warehouses at Puddle Dock and opened the Mermaid Theatre in 1959, the first theatre since actors had been evicted as rogues and vagabonds in 1619 by puritanical aldermen. After redevelopment the Mermaid reopened in 1981, its stage and auditorium enlarged, but now rather submerged beneath office blocks and marooned by the maelstrom of Upper Thames Street. Its future is secure, though Lord Miles may look back nostalgically on those heady impecunious days, nearly thirty years and 250 productions ago.

The Mermaid undoubtedly opened closed minds. The idea of incorporating a major new arts complex within the Barbican found increas-ing favour with the Corporation who finally decided in 1971 to commit vast sums for construction. Whatever the cost and criticisms ('impossible to find your way around', 'not enough ladies' loos', 'awful to park' . . .) the Arts Centre has transformed a housing estate into an exciting cultural arena drawing thousands of people every evening. The main hall, with plush wood panelling and myriad lights, is a base for the London Symphony Orchestra and English Chamber Orchestra – a staple of pot-boilers and excellent midday and early evening concerts. The magnificent theatre provides a long-awaited London home for the Royal Shakespeare Company – the best designed space combined with superb performing standards. The tiny Pit, the cinema, gallery, sculpture court and roof garden exist happily in the theatre's shadow. Neuroses about funding, audiences and competition with the South Bank are perpetual, but the Barbican Centre is here to stay.

The annual July City of London Festival propogates the arts City-wide. Livery halls, Middle Temple, Baltic Exchange and St. Bartholomew's Great Hall host concerts and exhibitions. Goldsmiths' Hall sponsor regular subscription concerts; lunchtime organ and chamber recitals enrich churches and the Bishopsgate Institute. The City of London Sinfonia spreads the word outside – the arts are alive in the City.

The annual City of London Festival offers much to nourish
the mind and body every July.

'The Shepherd and Sheep' in Paternoster Square, one of
many contributions to the arts commissioned by the City.

16
Fleet Street

Fleet Street is synonymous with journalism. In the narrow streets and lanes either side of Fleet Street on the western edge of the City most of the nation's daily and Sunday newspapers together with dozens of magazines and trade journals have been edited, printed and despatched. The Daily and Sunday Express, Daily Mail, The Sun, News of the World, Daily Mirror, Daily and Sunday Telegraph, Reuters and the Press Association all lie south of Holborn and west of Farringdon Street. The Financial Times is in Cannon Street, even closer to money-market news, and The Guardian is just half a mile up Farringdon Road, in socialist Islington. The Times, founded in 1785, moved out to Grays Inn Road in the 1970s and in 1985, to Wapping. From its old headquarters in Queen Victoria Street The Times held the unique record of never missing an issue, even during the worst of the Blitz.

English newspapers began in the City. The earliest, The Daily Courant and the Spectator, started life in Little Britain. Eighteenth-century London society thrived on news and gossip, to amuse the idle rich, to arouse the hot-headed gamblers, and to report events which might influence the decisions of City merchants and speculators. This combination of entertainment and information still applies.

The City has always been a centre of publishing and bookselling. Even after the Great Fire which destroyed their stock, the publishers and booksellers returned to their traditional quarter clustered around St. Paul's. Until 1940 most British publishers boasted an EC4 address. The wartime devastation forced many to the West End and Bloomsbury where houses 'temporarily' accommodated offices. They are still there. Genteel Mayfair is today's prestige location.

The newspaper industry has largely stayed despite the volatile world of tycoons angered by union stubbornness, the threat of non-unionised labour outside and new presses in Wapping. Many stories, one suspects, are simply good fodder for the leader writers. Fleet Street remains a curious juxtaposition of lawyers and journalists, fact and fiction, thronging during the morning with barristers and clerks, humming with hectic editors and printers in the late afternoons. Their co-existence coincides in the Wig and Pen or El Vino's where they share their penchant for a tipple.

Although Sogat '82 and the rest have agreed some technological innovations which affect the highest-paid manual workers in London, the smell of the side streets is as yet unchanged. Articulated lorries piled with giant rolls of Finnish newsprint squeeze between high buildings; expertly the paper is hoisted into the bowels of the printing machinery. The grimy walls are fly-posted with left-wing slogans and jazz venues – rather different from the boxing bouts advertised at Smithfield. During the afternoon, bundles of Evening Standards, hot off the press, are hurled from whirring rollers into delivery vans revving to tear off through the streets of London. Fleet Street lives on deadlines, always ready to change for a new lead story. At night when honest people are abed, this little corner of the City buzzes and jangles to bring you your morning paper.

Rising westwards from Ludgate Circus, Fleet Street is the traditional centre of journalism, but for how much longer?

17
Eating and Drinking

Eating and drinking is a serious business in the City, far exceeding the requirements of nutritional replenishment. While Lord Mayor's banquets and livery company dinners are heralded events, numerous feeding places and watering holes offer multifarious culinary and bibulous sustenance and foster face to face contact, both social and commercial – the basis of the City's power and prosperity.

One could spend years visiting every pub, restaurant and sandwich bar, by which time some would need re-inspection, having changed. Some institutions are seemingly inviolate, eternally popular. Simpson's Tavern founded in 1757 in an alley off Cornhill, is outstanding. Among wooden high-backed pews and polished racks for bowlers and brollies, a midday army of pin-striped gents enjoy basic English cooking – chump chops, bubble-and-squeak, stewed cheese and jam rolypoly – and no-nonsense molly-coddling by maternal waitresses. Nearby, in St. Michael's Alley, the Jamaica Wine House descends directly from the fashionable seventeenth-century coffee houses where business combined with pleasure. Waiters relayed financial transactions as well as serving refreshment. Gratuity boxes were inscribed 'T.I.P.' – to increase promptitude.

Although many pubs have been insensitively modernised with flock wallpaper, video games and canned music – ever vulnerable to whims of new landlords or brewery house-styles – a surprising number survive unspoilt in the City. The Hoop and Grapes, Aldgate High Street, boasts a continuous licence since 1300, and its Tudor timber frame and Jacobean brick facade pre-date the Great Fire. Old Wine Shades, Martin Lane, with its splendid external lantern and sign, was saved from demolition in 1972. These, together with Ye Olde Watling, Bow Lane, and the Horn, Knightrider Street, display low ceilings, blackened wood panelling, shuttered sash windows – smokily and pokily atmospheric. Even Dirty Dicks, Bishopsgate, is genuine beneath fake cobwebs and tawdry gimmickry.

The Old Cheshire Cheese, Fleet Street, remains hospitable despite Dr. Johnson's ghost, tourists, sawdust and hard seats. El Vino's, opposite, is famous for different reasons – clubby and prejudiced. Unpretentious simplicity – the East India Arms, Fenchurch Street, the Lamb, Leadenhall, the Magpie, New Street, or the Cock, Carter Lane, – is refreshing. Opulent Victorian gin-palaces survive at the Viaduct Tavern, Newgate, and the Lord Aberconway, Old Broad Street, with ornate balcony and superb cask beer.

Restaurants and cafés cater for most palates and pockets. Traditional chop-houses, like the George and Vulture, Castle Court, and the Throgmorton, exude brass and mahogany. The Bartholomew Grill is a closer reminder of how journeymen dined. The Fox and Anchor nearby satisfies Smithfield appetites with hearty breakfast blow-outs. Mersea Island oysters and lemon sole are washed down with muscadet at Gow's and Sweeting's. The Roux brothers' haute-cuisine at Le Gamin, Old Bailey, justifies the accolades – excellent if pricey. Gallipoli, tucked behind St. Botolph, Bishopsgate, was a Turkish bath, now a delightful restaurant, always busy. So is the basement Japanese refectory in Walbrook, packed with oriental bankers. New croissant bars and pizza parlours open regularly. Others disappear.

Souls of poets dead and gone,
What Elysium have ye known,
Happy field or mossy cavern,
Choicer than the Mermaid Tavern.

*A City favourite for those who like solid English cooking –
one of the hundreds of places to eat and drink in the City.*

Business, beer and sandwiches.

Lunchtime on the pedestrian walkway, high above the traffic on London Wall.

18
Statues and Memorials

Clues to the City's long history confront the keen-sighted at every turn. The wealth of statues, memorials, signs and curiosities provide the filigree which make the City so distinctive, the embellishments which every pedestrian should savour. How many centuries before the brave new worlds of Thamesmead or Docklands offer such microscopic fascination?

Statues abound in the City, a favourite contribution of Victorian worthies. The Queen, severe before St. Paul's steps, or Albert, coquettishly doffing his hat at Holborn Circus, are proudly eloquent. Rowland Hill, founder of the penny post, stands more contemplatively in King Edward Street, like the bust of George Peabody, housing philanthropist, behind the Royal Exchange. Several interesting monuments are anonymous. The stone Panyer Boy, carved in 1688, sits naked on a breadbasket near St. Paul's station where bakers sold their wares, and marks the City's summit: 'When ye have sought the City round, Yet still this is the highest ground.' At No.193 Fleet Street, a Byronesque sylph gazes wanly from above the shopfront. The charity boy and girl outside St. Andrew Holborn stare impassively.

The City churches contain many beautiful memorials – the exquisite portrait of Pepys' wife, Elizabeth, in St. Olave, and the reverential figure of John Stow in St. Andrew Undershaft whose hand-held quill is renewed annually by the Lord Mayor.

Modern sculpture enjoys special patronage in the City. 'Beyond Tomorrow' in Guildhall Yard and 'Shepherd and Sheep' in Paternoster Square stand poignant among monotony. The spindly 'Icarus' facing the neat spire of St. Nicholas Cole Abbey and the 'Minotaur' in Postman's Park, Little Britain, are aggressive examples of Michael Ayrton's mythology. Michael Black's memorial to Reuter at Royal Exchange is chunkily orthodox.

Future commissions could revive the traditional integration of sculpture with function. Ancient drinking fountains were lovingly decor-ated – the Aldgate pump at the Fenchurch/Leadenhall Street confluence, or the elegant fountain in Cornhill where a marble canopy shelters a bronze maiden. Sundials also inspire. In Pump Court, Middle Temple, the epitaph dates from 1686: 'Shadows we are and like shadows depart'. At dusk lamplighters ignite the old gas lanterns on their stays and posts.

Hanging signs and clocks in the streets display a host of hieroglyphics which puzzle and inform the passer-by. Gilded sunbeams in Basinghall Street, Britannia ringed by Greek letters in Coleman Street and the grasshopper outside Martin's Bank, Lombard Street, are emblems of insurance and banking, stretching back centuries. The giant ecclesiastical timepiece of St. Mary-le-Bow dominates Cheapside.

Numerous official blue plaques recall destroyed gates, churches and taverns, or identify the residences of famous people – Thomas à Becket, born at No. 86 Cheapside, John Keats born at his father's inn, the Swan and Hoop, now the Moorgate, Anton Bruckner who stayed in Finsbury Square in 1871, Benjamin Disraeli who worked in Fredericks Place off Old Jewry as a lad. Unofficial inscriptions augment this rich tabletry, like the fifty quaint obsequies to Victorian self-sacrifice in Postman's Park. Best are the smallest touches. On the corner of East-cheap and Philpot Lane two fossilised mice nibble among the delicate stone foliage.

Queen Victoria, before the steps of St. Paul's Cathedral.

The Cat and Fiddle; emblem of Martin's Bank.

19
Manhattan or Beyond?

Since 1945 the City has undergone enormous physical change. Nor does the pace of rebuilding slacken. Technological innovations and revolution in the banking and business world threaten even greater upheavals in the next decade.

The architectural face of the modern City has been moulded by three distinct post-war phases. Charred and flattened bomb sites offered the biggest opportunity for rebuilding since the conflagration of 1666, a chance which was grabbed enthusiastically in the 1950s and '60s. At the east end of the City the new totempole of the Nat-West Tower rose over the business quarter, surrounded by a phalanx of shiny glass and steel boxes. The Stock Exchange, 320 feet high, looms above the Bank of England. Richard Siefert and others ensured that the magnificent dome of St. Paul's, once London's dominant landmark, was overshadowed. Beside the cathedral Holford's unyielding blocks link Paternoster Square through to the Post Office redevelopment, London Wall and the Barbican. This is the 'futuristic' townscape of the 1960's planners, in reality a bleak spectre of windswept walkways, pedestrian concourses, stained concrete and faded cladding.

Sometimes the visual harshness of the worst inanity is offset by an exquisite gem nearby: a Wren church spire reflected in the bland glass of an anonymous curtain wall or a fragment of ragstone Roman fortification. At dusk the serried ranks of windows turn yellow, orange and red with the sinking sun, the top of the Nat-West Tower glinting after the rest have fallen into evening shadow.

Sparked off by tragedies like the vandalistic demolition of the splendid Coal Exchange in Lower Thames Street in 1962 a backlash of concern swept the City in the 1970s. 'Save the City' became the warcry of amenity societies, residents and, eventually, politicians. The Corporation designated twenty-one conservation areas to protect vulnerable historic districts such as Bow Lane, Carter Lane, Castle Court and Cloth Fair. It was resolved to seek the formal 'listing' (preservation) of every pre-war stone-fronted building in the City. The saving of Billingsgate, against the Corporation's wishes, and the rejection of the Mansion House scheme, after Ministerial intervention, seemed to drive the final nail into the comprehensive developers' coffin. Prince Charles' famous lambasting of Mies van der Rohe and Peter Palumbo's proposals for Mansion House Square – 'a giant glass stump better suited to Chicago' – summarised popular public opinion. Enough was enough.

New buildings in the late 1970s and early '80s fitted the conservationist image. The domestic scale of developments in Cloth Fair and the highly modelled 'City Village' in Lovat Lane harmonise with old buildings and historic street lines. The City Engineer was persuaded to scrap unwanted road-widening plans. Large, monolithic redevelopment was no longer to be tolerated. Besides, computerised terminals and automated word processors were, according to experts, reducing demand for large offices packed with filing clerks and typists. Refurbishment was a favoured, and often cheaper, alternative to redevelopment. Railway soot and grime were washed away to reveal sparkling marble and Portland stone. Victorian and Edwardian architecture became fashionable again.

After the insensitive belittling of St. Paul's, new policies now protect key views of the dome within the City and from distant vantage-points. Twenty years too late, many would claim, and unable to prevent the proposed 298 feet high pyramid for Bart's Hospital and Wimpeys behind the preserved Little Britain facade. Elsewhere, limited building heights have been respected. The slick high-tech offices by Covell Matthews Wheatley at Billingsgate and Ropemaker Street step each storey to avoid offence. Even Richard Rogers' dramatic Lloyd's building, with his inimitable external workings and metallic pipes, is closely hemmed in by older buildings, and fully blessed by the Royal Fine Arts Commission. The roof-top glass atrium,

window-cleaning cranes and gleaming stainless-steel air-conditioning ducts, resembling an outrageous motor-cycle engine, will amaze the airborne.

1985 shook the City to its roots. Canary Wharf in London's docklands proved that the re-development lull was temporary. Backed by American and Swiss finance, three massive towers, over 800 feet high, accommodating ten million square feet of new offices, and costing £1.5 billion, would launch a rival down-town

The top of the old Lloyd's building, overtaken in the quickening pace of redevelopment.

commercial centre for Europe, three miles east of the City. Suddenly, a seemingly insatiable appetite for huge new office spaces had emerged, crushing 'small is beautiful' wisdom. Deregulation and mergers on the Stock Exchange, take-overs forming gigantic corporations, and multi-national conglomerates combining bank-

The new Lloyd's building, the City's latest contribution to major post-war architecture, visually stunning both inside and out.

ing, broking, jobbing and insuring brazenly set out to undermine the City's foundations. London remains ideally placed within world time zones to trade with both America and Japan. But will the City, constrained by its old buildings and customs, be able to retain its monopoly, or be overwhelmed by competition outside?

Perhaps it was inevitable. The square mile had become the pinnacle of real estate in Britain, with rents per square foot reaching £40 per annum. To some extent, high rents were ploughed back into the City – money did not leave. What foreign investor, however, particularly with the magnitude of office floorspace envisaged at Canary Wharf, could fail to notice that beyond the City's eastern boundary land values plummet virtually to peppercorns? For some years, the City has been creeping into fringes of Clerkenwell, Southwark and Shoreditch, usually against the wishes of the adjacent boroughs. How attractive, then, the lure of Docklands, flaunting its colossal tax concessions, development grants, free rates and laissez-faire planning control.

Almost overnight, worried City officials scrabbled to make the City appear more attractive. A bullish pro-development lobby conjured extravagant ideas for roofing over London Wall. Renewed threats to the riverside, Bow Lane and Carter Lane may follow. No doubt the Mansion House scheme will raise its head, albeit in different perhaps more conventional clothing. Surplus buildings at Smithfield Market will be prime candidates.

The next decade will test many theories. How enduring are the centripetal forces which have sustained the City for so long? Will new satellite and video communications conspire with those who favour dispersal to loosen the close-knit community of the City? Will the City be panicked into over-hasty decisions for change? Will conservationists and public opinion accept a new spate of glass towers, either in the City or Dockland? Will the Nat-West Tower and the Stock Exchange in turn be dwarfed by a New York skyline? Can a middle path be trod between Manhattan and a museum? These are volatile times. But remember; new gadgets and development pressures will not quickly replace the instinctive human need to meet face to face, on the floor of Lloyd's, around the conference table, or over a pint of beer and a sandwich. The City, in the very heart of London, will continue to be the City.

*Cunard Place, in the heart of the City's central business
core where technological innovations and the 'big bang'
promise yet greater changes in the next decade.*

20
Cats and Caretakers

Quite properly this book has concentrated on those activities and institutions which make the City tick during the week, employing thousands of people who at the end of their working day leave for a domestic world elsewhere. In the evenings, at weekends and Bank Holidays a different City appears, known to those lucky enough to live there. John Betjeman, who lived in Cloth Fair, wrote nostalgically:

Sunday silence! with every street a dead street,
Alley and courtyard empty and cobbled mews,
Till 'tingle tang' the bell of St. Mildred's Bread Street
Summoned the sermon taster to high box pews.

Until the mid-nineteenth century the City was an important residential area, housing 100,000 people, albeit in chronically cramped conditions. In 1901 there were still 30,000 people living in the City, but this figure dwindled rapidly with rapacious commercial development and wartime evacuation. The customary distribution of food to the poor after the Lord Mayor's Banquet disappeared. By 1951 there were just 4,500, too few to sustain normal residential services. Nearly all the old City schools, such as Christ's Hospital and St. Paul's, have moved out to larger sites with playing fields and fresh air. The City of London Boys' and Girls' Schools remain, as does St. Paul's Choir School, beside its cathedral.

The completion in 1976 of 2,014 new dwellings in the Barbican and 181 flats in Middlesex Street, boosted the City's population to over 7,000.

Arguments continue about how many flats, particularly those that have been sold off, are used merely as hospitality suites or weekday pied-à-terres by company directors. At least one-third of Barbican residents have another home, a country retreat.

There are small residential enclaves in the Temple, Queenhythe and Cloth Fair, and nurses' hostels near St. Bartholomew's Hospital. Through the rest of the City are scattered the declining breed of tavern landlords and resident caretakers. Increasingly, pubs are run by managers who commute from outside; those which do open after work usually close early. Very few open at weekends. Live-in caretakers are being replaced by security firms with shift workers or roving patrols. The caretaker's flat becomes a penthouse used occasionally by livery company diners and board chairmen, or more office space.

The City is best explored when it is quiet. Narrow lanes which during the week resound with impatient footsteps, instil a sense of adventure, inviting the discovery of sequestered courts and hidden churchyards where lie the bones of long-dead Londoners. In the evenings, when the lubricated laughter of late-staying drinkers has trickled away to their last trains, the City becomes the domain of church mice and night owls. The main thoroughfares fall silent. Bright streetlamps blaze onto clean empty pavements, bathing stone and concrete in pink and orange. Traffic lights change and rechange. Down dark side alleys nothing stirs. Only, perhaps, a curtained glimmer in a high window or a sideways stare from a stealthy padding cat.

The tiny churchyard of St. Bride's, Fleet Street, a quiet refuge from the noise and bustle of the business world.

*The domes of Cannon Street station and St. Paul's, with
Mondial House in the foreground.*

Sunset from London Bridge.

Bibliography

Ash, R; *The Londoner's Almanac*, Century Publishing, 1985.

Betjeman, John; *The City of London Churches*, Pitkin, 1974.

Cathcart-Borer, M; *The City of London*, Constable, 1977.

Corporation of London; *City of London Local Plan*, City of London, 1986.

Forshaw, A. and Bergström, T; *Smithfield Past and Present*, Heinemann, 1980.

Forshaw, A. and Bergström, T.; *The Markets of London*, Penguin, 1986.

Forshaw, A. and Bergström, T; *The Open Spaces of London*, Allison & Busby, 1986.

Gibson-Jarvie, R; *The City of London: a financial and commercial history*, Woodhead-Faulkner, 1979.

Hearsey, John; *London and the Great Fire*, John Murray, 1965.

Hibbert, Christopher; *London: the Biography of a City*, Penguin, 1980.

Howgego, James L; *Victorian and Edwardian City of London*, Batsford, 1977.

Johnson, David; *The City Ablaze*, William Kimber, 1980.

Latham, R., (ed); *The Shorter Pepys*, Bell and Hyman, 1985.

Lloyd, David (ed); *Save the City*, Society for the Protection of Ancient Buildings/Civic Trust/ Victorian Society, 1976.

Milne, Gustav; *The Port of Roman London*, Batsford, 1985.

Morris, J; *Londinium*, Weidenfeld and Nicolson, 1982.

Norrie, I. (ed); *The Book of the City*, High Hill Books, 1961.

Pevsner, N; *The Buildings of England*; London, the cities of London and Westminster, 3rd Edition, Penguin, 1973.

Plender, J. and Wallace, P; *The Square Mile*, Hutchinson, 1985.

Rasmussen, S. E.; *London: the Unique City*, Pelican, 1960.

Stow, John; *The Survey of London*, 1st Edition, 1598.